D0752081

Citizenship
PASSING THE TEST

READY FOR THE INTERVIEW

Lynne Weintraub

New Readers Press
A Publishing Division of ProLiteracy

Sample sections of the Application for Naturalization used in this text are taken from
Form N-400 (Rev. 05/31/01) N, available from the United States Citizenship and Immigration Services.

Citizenship: Ready for the Interview
ISBN 978-1-56420-226-0

Copyright © 2002 New Readers Press
New Readers Press
A Publishing Division of ProLiteracy
1320 Jamesville Avenue, Syracuse, New York 13210
www.newreaderspress.com

Printed in the United States of America
9   8   7   6

All proceeds from the sale of New Readers Press materials
support literacy programs in the United States and worldwide.

Developmental Editor: Paula L. Schlusberg
Copy Editor: Judi Lauber
Production Director: Heather Witt
Designer: Kimbrly Koennecke
Cover Designer: Carolyn Wallace
Illustrators: Carolyn Wallace, Luciana Mallozzi, Linda Tiff, James P. Wallace
Production Specialist: Alexander Jones

Contents

Introduction

How to Use *Citizenship: Ready for the Interview*

Listen to This Information* 📻

When you apply for U.S. citizenship, you complete an application form. Later, you have an interview with an examiner with the USCIS, the U.S. Citizenship and Immigration Services. To do these things, you need to understand spoken English.

This book and the *Citizenship* audio recording can help you. Practice listening to the English words as you read along in the book. You will get more comfortable and confident as you practice.

The citizenship application is Form N-400, Application for Naturalization. You fill it out and send it to the USCIS.

Citizenship: Ready for the Interview can help you get ready to fill out the N-400 form. It shows how different people fill out their forms. And it lets you practice writing your own information on a blank form.

Later in the citizenship process, you will have an interview with a USCIS examiner. The examiner will
- ask questions about your application
- check if your answers match the answers on your application
- make sure you understand and speak English

Citizenship: Ready for the Interview can also help you prepare for the interview. You can
- hear and read sample interviews
- hear and read different ways examiners ask for the same information
- hear and read how different people answer interview questions
- think about how you will answer interview questions
- practice listening to questions and answering them in English

After lots of practice, we hope you will feel confident and ready for your interview. Good luck!

But remember—the citizenship process can change over time. Be sure you have the most recent N-400 form. And be sure you know the current requirements for citizenship. If you have questions, get advice from an immigration specialist.

When you see this symbol 📻, play the Citizenship *audio recording as you read along in the book.*

Applying for Citizenship

What to Expect at the Interview

Listen to the USCIS Examiner

Hello. My name is Mr. Cooper. I work at the U.S. Citizenship and Immigration Services (or USCIS). I'm a citizenship examiner.

Every day I interview many people. I ask the questions on the N-400 application. I check to see if there are any problems. I check to see if we need to make any changes in the application. I check to see if people are telling the truth.

Sometimes I look serious. I am trying to do my job quickly and carefully. Don't be afraid to talk to me.

If you don't understand a question, ask me to help you. Maybe I can repeat the question for you. Maybe I can ask the question in another way.

You need to speak and understand a little English. But it's OK if your English has some mistakes. You need to answer the questions, but you do not need to speak perfect English.

Are you getting ready for your interview? Read the questions on your N-400 application. Practice answering questions in English. If you practice, you will feel ready when you see me at the USCIS office.

Eligibility for Citizenship

Listen to the USCIS Examiner

To become a citizen you must be at least 18 years old. You must be a permanent resident. You must have a Permanent Resident Card, or a green card. If your husband or wife is already a citizen, you can become a citizen after three years. If you are not married to a citizen, you can become a citizen after five years.

You must pass a test of U.S. history and government.* Most people must also speak, read, and write a little English.

Be careful! If you have left the United States for more than six months, you may need to wait before you send your application. If you lied to USCIS to get your green card, there could be a problem. If you have ever been arrested or put in jail, there could be a problem.

And here is the most important thing: You must promise to make the United States your number one country. You must promise to help your new country if there is an emergency.

Some disabled people do not have to do this.

Benefits of Citizenship

Listen to Hai

I want to be a citizen for many reasons. If I become a citizen, I can vote in elections. I can bring my family here from Vietnam. I can get an American passport. I can get a job with the U.S. government.

Someday maybe I will need help from the government.* If I become a citizen, I can apply for this help.

What Will Hai Say?

Why do you want to be a citizen?

_____ **a.** Because I want to get welfare and food stamps.

_____ **b.** Because I want to get a green card and a job.

_____ **c.** Because this is my country. I want to stay in America.

Hai's Interview

EXAMINER: Why do you want to be a citizen?

HAI: Because this is my country now. I want to stay in America. And I want to vote.

What Will You Say?

Why do you want to be a citizen?

Some examples are food stamps, welfare, or financial aid for college.

Filling Out the N-400 Application

Listen to the USCIS Examiner 📻

When you fill out your N-400 form, you should print clearly. Use only CAPITAL letters. Use a black pen or a blue pen only.

Write your "A" number at the top of each page. This is the number on your Permanent Resident Card—your green card. The number begins with the letter "A." There should be nine numbers after the "A." If the "A" number has eight numbers, put a 0 before the first number.

You may still have an old green card. Or you may have a new card. The cards have different formats. But they both have your "A" number.

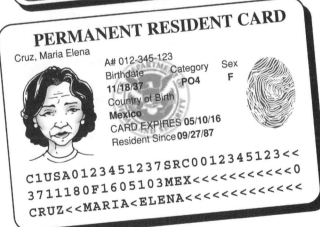

If you need more space to write any of your answers, use a separate piece of paper. At the top of the paper, write your name, your "A" number, and "N-400." Then write the number of the question you are answering.

Listen to Hai

 I am applying to be a citizen. My sister Lin wants to be a citizen too. We want to go to our interviews on the same day.

I wrote a note to USCIS:

> Dear USCIS,
> We would like to be interviewed on the same day, if it is possible.
> Hai Pham A#234567890
> Lin Pham A#234567891
>
> Thank you.
> Hai Pham
> Lin Pham

I said, "We would like to be interviewed on the same day, if it is possible.

Hai Pham A#234567890

Lin Pham A#234567891"

We put our applications together in one envelope.

Maybe our appointments will be on different days. But maybe USCIS will give us appointments on the same day. We hope that USCIS will be able to take us together.

The Application Process

Listen to Maria 📻

This year, I decided to apply for citizenship. I filled out an N-400 application. I wrote my "A" number at the top of each page. Then I signed the form.

I got photographs and a check to send with my application. I also sent a copy of the front and back of my green card. I made a copy of the application to keep for myself.

Soon, I got a letter back. It said my application arrived OK at USCIS.

Then I waited for an interview appointment. After many months, USCIS sent me an interview notice. The notice told me where and when to go for my interview.

U.S. Department of Homeland Security
United States Citizenship and Immigration Services

Notice of Naturalization Interview

United States Citizenship and Immigration Services		
DALLAS, TEXAS 75247	File or A# A 12 345 123	Date 11/17/2002

You are hereby notified to appear for an interview on your (your child's) application for naturalization at the DATE, TIME and PLACE, shown below.

Date 12/14/2002
Time 10:00 AM

Place   8101 N. STEMMONS FREEWAY
DALLAS, TX 75247
UNITED STATES CITIZENSHIP AND IMMIGRATION SERVICES

MARIA ELENA PEREZ

419 MAIN ST APT 122
DALLAS, TX 75208

I practiced for my interview. I looked at my N-400 application to remember the information. I listened to interview questions and practiced answering in English.

Today I will go to my interview. I decided to wear a nice dress. I remembered to bring my interview notice. I also have my passport, my green card, and my driver's license.

Now I am ready for my interview.

Getting Started at the Interview

Responding to Commands and Taking an Oath

Maria's Interview

Listen to the USCIS Examiner

 What will you do at your interview? Find a picture to go with the words.

1. Put your interview notice on the stack.
2. Please wait. Someone will call you.
3. Follow me.
4. Please come in.
5. Remain standing.
6. Raise your right hand.

7. You may sit down.
8. Show me your green card.
9. Please show me some identification.
10. Sign your name.

N-400 Part 1
Your Name

Your Current Legal Name

Listen to Maria

 My name is Maria Elena Perez. My last name is Perez. I'm Mrs. Perez. My husband was Mr. Perez. Perez is our family name.

My first name is Maria. Everyone calls me Maria. Maria is my given name.

My middle name is Elena.

Maria's Form

> **Part 1. Your Name** *(The Person Applying for Naturalization)*
>
> A. Your current legal name.
>
> Family Name *(Last Name)*
>
> **PEREZ**
>
> Given Name *(First Name)* | Full Middle Name *(If applicable)*
>
> **MARIA** | **ELENA**

What Will Maria Say?

So your family name is Perez. How do you spell it?

_____ **a.** Perez.

_____ **b.** P-E-R-E-Z.

_____ **c.** Maria Elena Perez.

Maria's Interview

EXAMINER: So your family name is Perez. How do you spell it?

MARIA: P-E-R-E-Z.

EXAMINER: OK. Your given name is Maria?

MARIA: Yes.

EXAMINER: And your middle name is, let's see . . . Elena—is that right?

MARIA: Yes.

Listen to Hai

My full name is Hai Pham. My family name is Pham. All of my brothers and sisters have the same family name. We are the Pham family.

My given name is Hai. I don't have a middle name.

Hai's Form

Part 1. Your Name *(The Person Applying for Naturalization)*

A. Your current legal name.

Family Name *(Last Name)*

> PHAM

Given Name *(First Name)*

> HAI

Full Middle Name *(If applicable)*

>

What Will Hai Say?

Could you state your full name, please?

_____ **a.** P-H-A-M.

_____ **b.** Full name.

_____ **c.** Hai Pham.

Hai's Interview

EXAMINER: Could you state your full name, please?

HAI: Hai Pham.

EXAMINER: Pham is the family name?

HAI: Yes.

EXAMINER: How do you spell it?

HAI: P-H-A-M.

EXAMINER: No middle name?

HAI: No.

What Will You Say?

State your full name, please.
What is your full name?

What's your family name?
What's your last name?

What's your first name?
What's your given name?

How do you spell that?
Could you spell your last name for me?

Do you have a middle name?
What's your middle name?

Your Form

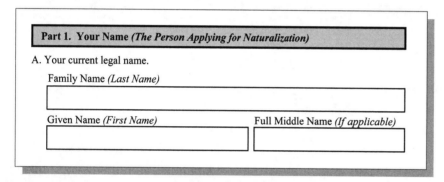

Part 1. Your Name *(The Person Applying for Naturalization)*

A. Your current legal name.

Family Name *(Last Name)*

Given Name *(First Name)*   Full Middle Name *(If applicable)*

The Name on Your Permanent Resident Card

Listen to Maria

My current legal name is Maria Elena Perez. That's the name I use now. That name goes in section A.

But my green card has a different name. Before I was married, my last name was Cruz. That's the name I used on my green card. In section B, I copied the name exactly as it is on my green card.

Maria's Form

> **Part 1. Your Name** *(The Person Applying for Naturalization)*
>
> A. Your current legal name.
>
> Family Name *(Last Name)*
>
> | PEREZ |
> |---|
>
> Given Name *(First Name)* | Full Middle Name *(If applicable)*
>
> | MARIA | ELENA |
> |---|---|
>
> B. Your name <u>exactly</u> as it appears on your Permanent Resident Card.
>
> Family Name *(Last Name)*
>
> | CRUZ |
> |---|
>
> Given Name *(First Name)* | Full Middle Name *(If applicable)*
>
> | MARIA | ELENA |
> |---|---|
>
> C. If you have ever used other names, provide them below.
>
> | Family Name *(Last Name)* | Given Name *(First Name)* | Middle Name |
> |---|---|---|
> | | | |
> | | | |
> | | | |

What Will Maria Say?

Your green card says "Maria Elena Cruz," right?

_____ **a.** No. My name is Maria.

_____ **b.** Yes.

_____ **c.** My last name is Perez.

Maria's Interview 🎙

EXAMINER: You are currently using a different name than the one on your Permanent Resident Card. Is that correct?

MARIA: I'm sorry. Can you say that more slowly?

EXAMINER: OK, your Permanent Resident Card—your green card—says Maria Elena Cruz, right?

MARIA: Yes.

EXAMINER: But you now use the name Maria Elena Perez.

MARIA: Yes, Perez. In the U.S. I use my married name, Perez.

Other Names

Listen to Hai

My name is Hai Pham. That is the name my mother and father gave to me. I have used that name since I was born. I have never used any other name.

Hai's Form

Part 1. Your Name *(The Person Applying for Naturalization)*

A. Your current legal name.

Family Name *(Last Name)*

PHAM

Given Name *(First Name)*	Full Middle Name *(If applicable)*
HAI	

B. Your name <u>exactly</u> as it appears on your Permanent Resident Card.

Family Name *(Last Name)*

PHAM

Given Name *(First Name)*	Full Middle Name *(If applicable)*
HAI	

C. If you have ever used other names, provide them below.

Family Name *(Last Name)*	Given Name *(First Name)*	Middle Name

What Will Hai Say?

Have you used any other names since you came here?

_____ **a.** No, just one name.

_____ **b.** Hai Pham.

_____ **c.** Yes, my name is Hai.

Hai's Interview

EXAMINER: Now, the name you've used here is Hai Pham. Have you used any other names since you came here?

HAI: No.

EXAMINER: You don't go by any other names?

HAI: Could you please repeat the question?

EXAMINER: Have you ever used another name?

HAI: No, just one name, all my life.

Listen to Nick

When I was born, my mother named me On Pick. My mother died when I was 7 years old. I came to America when I was 11 years old. I came here alone.

I lived with an American family, the Hill family. Later they adopted me, and I changed my name. Now I use an American name. My American name is Nick Hill.

Nick Hill is my legal name now. It's the name on my ID cards, and it's the name I use when I sign papers.

When I sent my application to USCIS, I sent a copy of my adoption papers.

Nick's Form

> **Part 1. Your Name** *(The Person Applying for Naturalization)*
>
> A. Your current legal name.
>
> Family Name *(Last Name)*
>
> | HILL |
>
> Given Name *(First Name)*   Full Middle Name *(If applicable)*
>
> | NICK | | |
>
> B. Your name <u>exactly</u> as it appears on your Permanent Resident Card.
>
> Family Name *(Last Name)*
>
> | PICK |
>
> Given Name *(First Name)*   Full Middle Name *(If applicable)*
>
> | ON | | |
>
> C. If you have ever used other names, provide them below.
>
> | Family Name *(Last Name)* | Given Name *(First Name)* | Middle Name |
> |---|---|---|
> | | | |
> | | | |
> | | | |

What Will Nick Say?

You seem to be using a different name than the one on your green card. Why is that?

_____ **a.** I changed my name.

_____ **b.** My name is Nick Hill.

_____ **c.** My green card has the name On Pick.

Nick's Interview

EXAMINER: Now, you seem to be using a different name than the one on your permanent resident card. Why is that?

NICK: I changed my name when I was adopted.

EXAMINER: So Nick Hill is your current legal name?

NICK: Current?

EXAMINER: Is Nick Hill your legal name now?

NICK: Yes.

Listen to Lisa

My Chinese name is Xia-Zheng Chen. My passport and my green card say Xia-Zheng Chen. That's my current legal name. But in the United States some people have trouble saying my name. So now I use the name Lisa Chen.

Lisa's Form

Part 1. Your Name *(The Person Applying for Naturalization)*

A. Your current legal name.

Family Name *(Last Name)*

CHEN

Given Name *(First Name)*	Full Middle Name *(If applicable)*
XIA-ZHENG	

B. Your name <u>exactly</u> as it appears on your Permanent Resident Card.

Family Name *(Last Name)*

CHEN

Given Name *(First Name)*	Full Middle Name *(If applicable)*
XIA-ZHENG	

C. If you have ever used other names, provide them below.

Family Name *(Last Name)*	Given Name *(First Name)*	Middle Name
CHEN	**LISA**	

What Will Lisa Say?

Have you ever gone to court to change your name?

_____ **a.** No.

_____ **b.** It's easier to say.

_____ **c.** L-I-S-A.

Lisa's Interview

EXAMINER: You have two names listed on your application form, Xia-Zheng Chen and Lisa Chen. What is the reason for that?

LISA: My Chinese name is Xia-Zheng. But I use the name Lisa in the U.S. because Lisa is easier for some people to say.

EXAMINER: Which one is your legal name?

LISA: Legal?

EXAMINER: Have you gone to court to change your name to Lisa Chen?

LISA: No.

EXAMINER: Then Xia-Zheng Chen is your legal name, for now.

What Will You Say?

Please state your full legal name.

What is your current legal name?

Have you used any other names since you came here?

Have you used any other names since you became a permanent resident?

Do you go by any other names?

What other names have you used?

Have you ever changed your name?

Your Form

Part 1. Your Name *(The Person Applying for Naturalization)*

A. Your current legal name.

Family Name *(Last Name)*

Given Name *(First Name)*   Full Middle Name *(If applicable)*

B. Your name <u>exactly</u> as it appears on your Permanent Resident Card.

Family Name *(Last Name)*

Given Name *(First Name)*   Full Middle Name *(If applicable)*

C. If you have ever used other names, provide them below.

Family Name *(Last Name)*	Given Name *(First Name)*	Middle Name

Name Change

Listen to Lisa

When you become a citizen, you can take a new name. I want my citizenship papers to say Lisa Xia-Zheng Chen. I want to change my name.

Lisa's Form

D. Name change *(optional)*

Please read the Instructions before you decide whether to change your name.

1. Would you like to legally change your name?　　☑ Yes　　☐ No
2. If "Yes," print the new name you would like to use. Do not use initials or abbreviations when writing your new name.

Family Name *(Last Name)*

CHEN

Given Name *(First Name)*	Full Middle Name
LISA	XIA-ZHENG

What Will Lisa Say?

What name do you want to use after you become a citizen?

_____ **a.** Yes, I do.

_____ **b.** Next year.

_____ **c.** Lisa Xia-Zheng Chen.

Lisa's Interview

EXAMINER: Your application says you want to change your name. What name do you want to use after you become a citizen?

LISA: Lisa Xia-Zheng Chen.

Listen to Hai

I don't want a new name. I want to keep my name the same.

Hai's Form

D. Name change *(optional)*

Please read the Instructions before you decide whether to change your name.

1. Would you like to legally change your name? ☐ Yes ☑ No

2. If "Yes," print the new name you would like to use. Do not use initials or abbreviations when writing your new name.

Family Name *(Last Name)*

Given Name *(First Name)* | Full Middle Name

What Will Hai Say?

Do you want to change your name?

_____ **a.** No, I don't.

_____ **b.** Hai Pham.

_____ **c.** Yes, the same.

Hai's Interview

EXAMINER: Some people change their names when they become U.S. citizens. Do you want to change your name?

HAI: No, I don't.

What Will You Say? 📻

Do you want to change your name?
Would you like to change your name?

What name do you want to use when you become a citizen?
What name do you want on your naturalization certificate?

Your Form

D. Name change *(optional)*

Please read the Instructions before you decide whether to change your name.

1. Would you like to legally change your name? ☐ Yes ☐ No

2. If "Yes," print the new name you would like to use. Do not use initials or abbreviations when writing your new name.

Family Name *(Last Name)*

Given Name *(First Name)*	Full Middle Name

N-400 Part 2
Information about Your Eligibility

Listen to Maria

To become a citizen you have to be a lawful permanent resident for five years or longer. I have been a permanent resident since 1987. I came to the U.S. in 1987. I got my green card more than five years ago.

Maria's Form

Part 2. Information About Your Eligibility *(Check Only One)*

I am at least 18 years old **AND**

A. ☑ I have been a Lawful Permanent Resident of the United States for at least 5 years.

B. ☐ I have been a Lawful Permanent Resident of the United States for at least 3 years, AND
I have been married to and living with the same U.S. citizen for the last 3 years, AND
my spouse has been a U.S. citizen for the last 3 years.

C. ☐ I am applying on the basis of qualifying military service.

D. ☐ Other *(Please explain)* _____

_____

What Will Maria Say?

How long have you been a permanent resident?

_____ **a.** Since 1987.

_____ **b.** I have a green card.

_____ **c.** Yes, I am.

Maria's Interview

EXAMINER: Let's see. You've been a permanent resident since 1987.
Is that right?

MARIA: Permanent resident? Can you say it again?

EXAMINER: How long have you been a permanent resident?

MARIA: Oh. Since 1987.

Listen to Susan

Three years ago, I married a U.S. citizen. I am still married. I have been married to a citizen for three years.

Three years ago, I got my green card. I have been a permanent resident for three years. I have lived in the U.S. with my husband for the whole three years.

I can apply for citizenship after only three years.

Susan's Form

Part 2. Information About Your Eligibility *(Check Only One)*

I am at least 18 years old **AND**

A. ☐ I have been a Lawful Permanent Resident of the United States for at least 5 years.

B. ☑ I have been a Lawful Permanent Resident of the United States for at least 3 years, AND I have been married to and living with the same U.S. citizen for the last 3 years, AND my spouse has been a U.S. citizen for the last 3 years.

C. ☐ I am applying on the basis of qualifying military service.

D. ☐ Other *(Please explain)* _____

_____

What Will Susan Say?

You've been a permanent resident for three years, is that right?

_____ **a.** Yes.

_____ **b.** Permanent resident.

_____ **c.** 1996.

Susan's Interview

EXAMINER: You've been a permanent resident for three years, is that right?

SUSAN: Yes.

EXAMINER: So you're eligible for citizenship based on marriage to a citizen.

SUSAN: Yes.

EXAMINER: How long have you been married?

SUSAN: Three years.

EXAMINER: And you're still married? No change?

SUSAN: Yes, I'm still married.

EXAMINER: When did your husband become a citizen?

SUSAN: In 1998.

EXAMINER: Do you currently live with your husband?

SUSAN: Yes.

EXAMINER: And you've lived with him continuously since you were married?

SUSAN: Continuously?

EXAMINER: Did you live with him the whole time—for the full three years?

SUSAN: Yes, that's right.

What Will You Say?

How long have you been a permanent resident?
How many years have you had your green card?
How many years have you had your permanent resident card?

When did you become a permanent resident?
When did you get your permanent resident card?

Questions for a Woman Married to a Citizen

– Is your application based on marriage to a citizen?
– How long has your husband been a citizen?
– When did your husband become a citizen?– Are you currently married?
– When did you get married?
– Are you still married?
– How long have you been married?
– Are you still living with your husband?
– How long have you lived with your husband?
– Have you lived with your husband continuously for the last three years?

Questions for a Man Married to a Citizen

– Is your application based on marriage to a citizen?
– How long has your wife been a citizen?
– When did your wife become a citizen?
– Are you currently married?
– When did you get married?
– Are you still married?
– How long have you been married?
– Are you still living with your wife?
– How long have you lived with your wife?
– Have you lived with your wife continuously for the last three years?

Your Form

Part 2. Information About Your Eligibility *(Check Only One)*

I am at least 18 years old **AND**

A. ☐ I have been a Lawful Permanent Resident of the United States for at least 5 years.

B. ☐ I have been a Lawful Permanent Resident of the United States for at least 3 years, AND I have been married to and living with the same U.S. citizen for the last 3 years, AND my spouse has been a U.S. citizen for the last 3 years.

C. ☐ I am applying on the basis of qualifying military service.

D. ☐ Other *(Please explain)* _____

N-400 Part 3
Information about You

Basic Information

Listen to Hai

I wrote my Social Security number and my date of birth on my application.

In the U.S., people write the month first, the day next, and the year last. My date of birth is November 7, 1969. I wrote the date like this: 11/07/1969.

The date I became a permanent resident was July 8, 1993. I wrote the date like this: 07/08/1993.

Hai's Form

Part 3. Information About You

A. Social Security Number

127-40-1837

B. Date of Birth *(Month/Day/Year)*

11/07/1969

C. Date You Became a Permanent Resident *(Month/Day/Year)*

07/08/1993

What Will Hai Say?

Your date of birth is November 7, 1967, is that correct?

_____ **a.** No, it's 1969.

_____ **b.** No, my Social Security number.

_____ **c.** No, in Vietnam.

Hai's Interview

EXAMINER: What's your Social Security number?

HAI: 127-40-1837.

EXAMINER: And your date of birth is November 7, 1967, is that correct?

HAI: No, it's 1969.

EXAMINER: 1969 . . . OK.

Listen to Hai

If you look carefully on your green card, you can find the date you became a permanent resident. I came to the U.S. as a refugee on July 8, 1993. I became a permanent resident on the day I arrived in the U.S.

Hai's Green Card

```
          ALIEN REGISTRATION RECEIPT CARD
PERSON IDENTIFIED BY THIS CARD IS ENTITLED TO RESIDE PERMANENTLY IN THE U.S.




 P26  SFO  930708  245  1158012001

 A1USA234567890<01<9107<<<<<<<
 6911077F0107172<<<<<<86006DE37
 PHAM>HAI<<<<<<<<<<<<<<<<<<<<<
```

Hai's Form

C. Date You Became a Permanent Resident *(Month/Day/Year)*

07/08/1993

Listen to Maria

I came to the U.S. as an immigrant on September 27, 1987. I became a permanent resident on the day I arrived in the U.S.

Maria's Green Card

PERMANENT RESIDENT CARD

Resident Since **09/27/87**

```
C1USA0123451237SRC0012345123<<
3711180F1605103MEX<<<<<<<<<<0
CRUZ<<MARIA<ELENA<<<<<<<<<<<
```

Maria's Form

C. Date You Became a Permanent Resident *(Month/Day/Year)*

09/27/1987

Listen to Chong 📻

 I came to the U.S. as a tourist in 1989. I did not have a green card then. I was not a permanent resident. In 1993 I got an adjustment of status. That's when I became a permanent resident. That's when I got my green card.

Chong's Green Card

ALIEN REGISTRATION RECEIPT CARD
PERSON IDENTIFIED BY THIS CARD IS ENTITLED TO RESIDE PERMANENTLY IN THE U.S.

```
P26  WAS  930607  245  1158012001

A1USA098765432<01<9107<<<<<<<
7002147F0107172<<<<<<86006DE37
BARTON>CHONG<<<<<<<<<<<<<<<<<<
```

Chong's Form

C. Date You Became a Permanent Resident *(Month/Day/Year)*

06/07/1993

What Will Chong Say?

When did you get your green card?
_____ **a.** In Los Angeles.
_____ **b.** Permanent resident.
_____ **c.** In 1993.

Chong's Interview 📻

EXAMINER: When you arrived in the United States, you were not a permanent resident. Is that right?

CHONG: Yes. I came on a tourist visa.

EXAMINER: When did you get an adjustment of status?

CHONG: What did you say?

EXAMINER: When did you become a permanent resident? When did you get your green card?

CHONG: Uh . . . that was in 1993.

What Will You Say? 📻

Do you know your Social Security number?
What is your Social Security number?

What's your date of birth?
When were you born?

Can you tell me the date you became a permanent resident?
When did you become a permanent resident?
When did you get your green card?

Your Form

| Part 3. Information About You |

A. Social Security Number

_ _ _ - _ _ - _ _ _ _

B. Date of Birth *(Month/Day/Year)*

_ _ / _ _ / _ _ _ _

C. Date You Became a Permanent Resident *(Month/Day/Year)*

_ _ / _ _ / _ _ _ _

Country of Birth/Country of Nationality

Listen to Maria

I was born in Mexico. Mexico is my country of birth. I am a citizen of Mexico right now. My country of nationality is Mexico.

Maria's Form

D. Country of Birth	E. Country of Nationality
MEXICO	MEXICO

What Will Maria Say?

So you're a citizen of Mexico?

_____ **a.** My country.

_____ **b.** I want to be a U.S. citizen.

_____ **c.** That's right.

Maria's Interview

EXAMINER: What's your country of nationality?

MARIA: Mexico.

EXAMINER: So you are a citizen of Mexico?

MARIA: Yes, that's right.

Listen to Nick

I was born in a refugee camp in Thailand. But I am not a citizen of Thailand.

My parents were from Cambodia. I am Cambodian. Cambodia is my country of nationality.

Nick's Form

D. Country of Birth	E. Country of Nationality
THAILAND	**CAMBODIA**

What Will Nick Say?

Is Thailand your country of nationality?

_____ **a.** No, I'm a Cambodian citizen.

_____ **b.** Yes, I was born in Thailand.

_____ **c.** I want to be an American.

Nick's Interview

EXAMINER: Your application says you were born in Thailand.

NICK: Yes, that's right.

EXAMINER: Is Thailand your country of nationality?

NICK: No, I'm a Cambodian citizen.

Listen to Sergei

I was born in the Soviet Union. Now there is no Soviet Union. But I wrote Soviet Union on my form anyway. The Soviet Union is still my country of birth.

I am a citizen of Russia. That's the name of my country now. My country of nationality is Russia.

Sergei's Form

D. Country of Birth	E. Country of Nationality
SOVIET UNION	RUSSIA

What Will Sergei Say?

Now, you were born in the Soviet Union, is that right?

_____ **a.** My country.

_____ **b.** I want to be a U.S. citizen.

_____ **c.** Yes, in the Soviet Union. That's right.

Sergei's Interview

EXAMINER: Now you were born in the Soviet Union, is that right?

SERGEI: Yes, in the Soviet Union. That's right.

EXAMINER: What's your country of nationality?

SERGEI: Russia.

EXAMINER: So, you're a Russian citizen.

SERGEI: Yes.

Listen to Celia

My father became a U.S. citizen many years ago, but he returned to Portugal. I was born in Portugal. After I came to America, I decided to apply for citizenship. I talked to an immigration expert about my application. He asked questions about my family and looked at my papers. Then he gave me a big surprise. He told me that I am a U.S. citizen now!

If your mother or father is (or was) a citizen, check with an immigration expert. You might be a U.S. citizen already.

Celia's Form

F. Are either of your parents U.S. citizens? *(if yes, see Instructions)* ☑ Yes ☐ No

What Will You Say?

What is your country of birth?
Where were you born?
In which country were you born?

What is your country of nationality?
Are you a citizen of any other country?

Is your mother or your father a U.S. citizen?
Are either of your parents U.S. citizens?

Your Form

D. Country of Birth

E. Country of Nationality

F. Are either of your parents U.S. citizens? *(if yes, see Instructions)* ☐ Yes ☐ No

Marital Status

Listen to Maria

My husband died in 1997. I am not married anymore. I am a widow.

Maria's Form

G. What is your current marital status? ☐ Single, Never Married ☐ Married ☐ Divorced ☑ Widowed

☐ Marriage Annulled or Other *(Explain)* _____

What Will Maria Say?

What is your marital status?
_____ **a.** My husband's family.
_____ **b.** In 1997.
_____ **c.** I'm a widow.

Maria's Interview

EXAMINER: What is your marital status?
MARIA: Uh . . . marital?
EXAMINER: Are you currently married? Divorced?
MARIA: I'm a widow. My husband died in 1997.
EXAMINER: I'm sorry to hear that, Mrs. Perez.

Listen to Chong

I got married when I was very young. But my husband and I were not happy together. We decided to get a divorce. I am not married anymore. I am divorced.

Chong's Form

G. What is your current marital status?　☐ Single, Never Married　☐ Married　☑ Divorced　☐ Widowed

☐ Marriage Annulled or Other *(Explain)* _____

What Will Chong Say?

You're divorced, right?

_____ **a.** No, I'm not married.

_____ **b.** Ten years ago.

_____ **c.** Yes, I'm divorced.

Chong's Interview

EXAMINER: You're divorced, right?

CHONG:　　Yes, I'm divorced.

Listen to Hai

 I have never been married. I don't have a wife. I am single.

Hai's Form

G. What is your current marital status?   ☑ Single, Never Married   ☐ Married   ☐ Divorced   ☐ Widowed

☐ Marriage Annulled or Other *(Explain)* _____

What Will Hai Say?

Have you ever been married?

_____ **a.** Yes. I'm single.

_____ **b.** No.

_____ **c.** Maybe someday.

Hai's Interview

EXAMINER: What's your marital status?

HAI: Excuse me. Could you ask it in another way?

EXAMINER: Are you currently married?

HAI: No, I'm single.

EXAMINER: Have you ever been married?

HAI: No.

Listen to Susan

I am married. I have a husband.

Susan's Form

G. What is your current marital status? ☐ Single, Never Married ☑ Married ☐ Divorced ☐ Widowed

☐ Marriage Annulled or Other *(Explain)* _____

What Will Susan Say?

What's your marital status?

_____ **a.** Yes. My husband.

_____ **b.** No.

_____ **c.** I'm married.

Susan's Interview

EXAMINER: What's your marital status?

SUSAN: I'm married.

Waivers and Accommodations

Listen to Hai

My sister Lin is disabled. It is very hard for her to learn new things. She forgets many things I tell her. Her doctor says that she will always need special help.

When I applied to become a citizen, Lin wanted to be a citizen too. So Lin's doctor filled out a form called N-648. The doctor explained the medical reasons for Lin's problem. She explained why Lin cannot study for a test. If the USCIS examiner agrees with the doctor, Lin will not have to take a test. I will help her when she has her interview. She will become a citizen too.

Lin's Form

H. Are you requesting a waiver of the English and/or U.S. History and Government requirements based on a disability or impairment and attaching a Form N-648 with your application? ☑Yes ☐No

Listen to Otto

I am 72 years old. My ears are not strong anymore. Sometimes I cannot hear what people say to me. I have been getting ready for my interview for a long time. But I do not know if I will be able to hear the examiner's questions. I'm asking for a small change in the way the examiner does the interview.

If you have a disability, you can write about it in your application. You can suggest a way for the examiner to make the interview easier for you. You can ask for an accommodation.

I am asking the examiner to let my daughter go with me to my interview. If I cannot hear a question, my daughter will repeat the question close to my ear. Sometimes I can hear my daughter better than I can hear other people.

Otto's Form

I. Are you requesting an accommodation to the naturalization process because of a disability or impairment? *(See Instructions for some examples of accommodations.)* ☑Yes ☐No

If you answered "Yes", check the box below that applies:

☐ I am deaf or hearing impaired and need a sign language interpreter who uses the following language: _____

☐ I use a wheelchair.

☐ I am blind or sight impaired.

☑ I will need another type of accommodation. Please explain: I HAVE TROUBLE HEARING SOME PEOPLE. PLEASE ALLOW MY DAUGHTER TO ACCOMPANY ME TO MY INTERVIEW. IF I CANNOT HEAR A QUESTION, SHE WILL REPEAT IT IN MY EAR.

N-400 Part 4
Addresses and Telephone Numbers

Home Address

Listen to Maria

I live in an apartment building. It's at 419 Main Street. My home address is 419 Main Street. That's where I get my mail. My apartment number is 122.

Maria's Form

Part 4. Addresses and Telephone Numbers	
A. Home Address - Street Number and Name *(Do NOT write a P.O. Box in this space)*	Apartment Number
419 MAIN ST.	122

What Will Maria Say?

What's your current address?

_____ **a.** Texas.

_____ **b.** 419 Main Street, Apartment 122.

_____ **c.** I live in an apartment.

Maria's Interview

EXAMINER: What's your current address?

MARIA: Uh . . . current?

EXAMINER: What is your address right now?

MARIA: 419 Main Street, Apartment 122.

Listen to Susan

I live in Bridgeport, Connecticut. My city is Bridgeport. But I didn't know what county Bridgeport is in.

If you don't know, you have to ask somebody. I asked my neighbor, but she didn't know either. Then I asked the mailman. He told me Bridgeport is in Fairfield County. He told me how to spell it: F-A-I-R-F-I-E-L-D.

Bridgeport is in Connecticut. Connecticut is my state. I know my zip code. It's 01048.

Susan's Form

Part 4. Addresses and Telephone Numbers

A. Home Address - Street Number and Name *(Do NOT write a P.O. Box in this space)* | Apartment Number

37 LINCOLN ST.

City	County	State	ZIP Code	Country
BRIDGEPORT	FAIRFIELD	CT	01048	USA

What Will Susan Say?

Do you still live in Bridgeport, Connecticut?

_____ **a.** Yes, Bridgeport.

_____ **b.** Fairfield County.

_____ **c.** My city and state.

Susan's Interview

EXAMINER: Do you still live in Bridgeport, Connecticut?
SUSAN: Yes, Bridgeport.
EXAMINER: So that's . . . Fairfield County?
SUSAN: Yes, Fairfield County.

Mailing Address/Telephone Numbers/E-mail Address

Listen to Hai 🔊

It's important to write your address clearly on your application. If your address changes later on, you have to tell USCIS your new address. USCIS needs to know where to send your interview notice.

My mailing address is the same as my street address. I don't have a post office box. My phone number at home is (510) 233-9888. My phone number at work is (510) 233-4295. I don't have an e-mail address.

Hai's Form

> **Part 4. Addresses and Telephone Numbers**
>
> A. Home Address - Street Number and Name *(Do NOT write a P.O. Box in this space)*   Apartment Number
>
> **3235 NORTH 58TH ST.**   **D-5**
>
> City | County | State | ZIP Code | Country
> **OAKLAND** | **ALAMEDA** | **CA** | **94649** | **USA**
>
> B. Care of   Mailing Address - Street Number and Name *(If different from home address)*   Apartment Number
>
> **N/A**
>
> City   State   ZIP Code   Country
>
> C. Daytime Phone Number *(If any)*   Evening Phone Number *(If any)*   E-mail Address *(If any)*
>
> **(510) 233-4295**   **(510) 233-9888**   **N/A**

What Will Hai Say?

Is there an apartment number?

_____ **a.** Yes, Apartment D-5.

_____ **b.** Yes, 3235 North 58th Street.

_____ **c.** Yes, I live in an apartment.

Hai's Interview 🔊

EXAMINER: Is this address still current, 3235 North 58th Street?

HAI: Yes, that's right.

EXAMINER: Is there an apartment number?

HAI: Yes, Apartment D-5.

EXAMINER: And what is your phone number?

HAI: (510) 233-9888.

Listen to Lisa

I have two addresses. I live at 154 Glendale Avenue. That's my street address. But I get my mail at the post office. My mailing address is P.O. Box 1658.

I have two phone numbers, one at work and one at home. I have an e-mail address too. I wrote them all on the form.

Lisa's Form

Part 4. Addresses and Telephone Numbers

A. Home Address - Street Number and Name *(Do NOT write a P.O. Box in this space)*   Apartment Number

154 GLENDALE AVE.

City	County	State	ZIP Code	Country
RIVERDALE	MORRIS	NJ	07457	USA

B. Care of   Mailing Address - Street Number and Name *(If different from home address)*   Apartment Number

P.O. BOX 1658

City	State	ZIP Code	Country
RIVERDALE	NJ	07457	USA

C. Daytime Phone Number *(If any)*   Evening Phone Number *(If any)*   E-mail Address *(If any)*

(973) 842-9090   (973) 825-4193   lisa@eslnet.com

What Will Lisa Say?

What is your street address?
_____ **a.** P.O. Box 1658.
_____ **b.** Riverdale, New Jersey.
_____ **c.** 154 Glendale Avenue.

Lisa's Interview

EXAMINER: Are you still receiving mail at P.O. Box 1658?
LISA: Yes.
EXAMINER: And what is your street address?
LISA: 154 Glendale Avenue, Riverdale, New Jersey.
EXAMINER: Is that in Passaic County?
LISA: No. It's Morris County.

What Will You Say? 📻

Where do you live?
What is your current address?
What is your street address?

What is your city?
What city do you live in?

What is your state?
What state are you in?

What's your zip code?

Which county is that?

Has your address changed since you sent in your application?

Do you have a different mailing address?
What's your mailing address?
Where do you receive mail?

What's your phone number?
Do you have a different number at work?

Do you have an e-mail address?

Your Form

Part 4. Addresses and Telephone Numbers

A. Home Address - Street Number and Name *(Do NOT write a P.O. Box in this space)*   Apartment Number

City   County   State   ZIP Code   Country

B. Care of   Mailing Address - Street Number and Name *(If different from home address)*   Apartment Number

City   State   ZIP Code   Country

C. Daytime Phone Number *(If any)*   Evening Phone Number *(If any)*   E-mail Address *(If any)*
(   )   (   )

N-400 Part 5
Information for Criminal Records Search

Listen to Hai

When you apply to become a citizen, USCIS checks your fingerprints. They need information to go with your fingerprints. You put that information in Part 5 of your application.

Tell if you are a man or a woman. Tell how tall you are and how much you weigh. Tell whether you are white, Asian, black, or Native American. And tell your eye color and hair color.

These questions are on the application, but the examiner will not ask them at your interview.

Hai's Form

Part 5. Information for Criminal Records Search

Note: The categories below are those required by the FBI. See Instructions for more information.

A. Gender
  ☑ Male   ☐ Female

B. Height
  5 Feet **8** Inches

C. Weight
  167 Pounds

D. Race
  ☐ White   ☑ Asian or Pacific Islander   ☐ Black   ☐ American Indian or Alaskan Native   ☐ Unknown

E. Hair color
  ☑ Black   ☐ Brown   ☐ Blonde   ☐ Gray   ☐ White   ☐ Red   ☐ Sandy   ☐ Bald (No Hair)

F. Eye color
  ☑ Brown   ☐ Blue   ☐ Green   ☐ Hazel   ☐ Gray   ☐ Black   ☐ Pink   ☐ Maroon   ☐ Other

---

Your Form

Part 5. Information for Criminal Records Search

Note: The categories below are those required by the FBI. See Instructions for more information.

A. Gender

☐ Male   ☐ Female

B. Height

Feet	Inches

C. Weight

	Pounds

D. Race

☐ White   ☐ Asian or Pacific Islander   ☐ Black   ☐ American Indian or Alaskan Native   ☐ Unknown

E. Hair color

☐ Black   ☐ Brown   ☐ Blonde   ☐ Gray   ☐ White   ☐ Red   ☐ Sandy   ☐ Bald (No Hair)

F. Eye color

☐ Brown   ☐ Blue   ☐ Green   ☐ Hazel   ☐ Gray   ☐ Black   ☐ Pink   ☐ Maroon   ☐ Other

N-400 Part 6
Your Residence and Employment

Residence

Listen to Hai 🔊

I have lived at the same address since October 1994. In the last five years, I had only one address.

Hai's Form

Part 6. Information About Your Residence and Employment

A. Where have you lived during the last 5 years? Begin with where you live now and then list every place you lived for the last 5 years. If you need more space, use a separate sheet of paper.

Street Number and Name, Apartment Number, City, State, Zip Code and Country	Dates *(Month/Year)*	
	From	To
Current Home Address - Same as Part 4.A	1 0 / 1 9 9 4	Present
	_ _ / _ _ _ _	_ _ / _ _ _ _

What Will Hai Say?

You live at 3235 North 58th Street, right?

_____ **a.** No. I don't.

_____ **b.** 8 years in Oakland.

_____ **c.** Yes, 3235 North 58th Street.

Hai's Interview 🔊

EXAMINER: Now, Mr. Pham, could you tell me how long you've been at your current residence?

HAI: What do you mean?

EXAMINER: You live at 3235 North 58th Street, right?

HAI: Yes.

EXAMINER: How long have you lived there?

HAI: Since 1995, I think. . . . No—since 1994.

EXAMINER: 1994?

HAI: Yes, since 1994.

Listen to Susan

I have moved three times in the last five years. I wrote all three addresses in Part 6.

Susan's Form

<table>
<tr><td colspan="3">Part 6. Information About Your Residence and Employment</td></tr>
</table>

A. Where have you lived during the last 5 years? Begin with where you live now and then list every place you lived for the last 5 years. If you need more space, use a separate sheet of paper.

Street Number and Name, Apartment Number, City, State, Zip Code and Country	Dates (Month/Year) From	To
Current Home Address - Same as Part 4.A	06,2001	Present
25 BEDFORD COURT, TEANECK, NJ 07105 U.S.A.	12,2000	06,2001
101 SOUTH MAIN ST., NEWARK, NJ 07666 U.S.A.	04,1998	12,2000
KINGSTON, JAMAICA	01,1987	04,1998
	__/____	__/____

What Will Susan Say?

How long have you lived at your current address?
_____ **a.** Since June 2001.
_____ **b.** Yes, I did.
_____ **c.** Bridgeport, Connecticut.

Susan's Interview

EXAMINER: How long have you lived at your current address?
SUSAN: Since June 2001.
EXAMINER: What was your previous address?
SUSAN: Excuse me?
EXAMINER: What was your address before you lived in Bridgeport?
SUSAN: 25 Bedford Court, Teaneck, New Jersey.
EXAMINER: When did you begin living at that address?
SUSAN: In late 2000.
EXAMINER: Have you lived anywhere else in the last five years?
SUSAN: Yes. I lived in Newark, New Jersey, and before that I lived in Jamaica.

What Will You Say? 📻

How long have you lived at your current address?
How long have you lived at this address?
How long have you lived where you are now?

What was your previous address?
What was your last address?
Where did you live before?

When did you begin living at that address?
When did you move to that address?
When did you leave that address?

Have you lived anywhere else in the last five years?
Have you lived at any other addresses?
Where else have you lived since you became a permanent resident?

Your Form

Part 6. Information About Your Residence and Employment

A. Where have you lived during the last 5 years? Begin with where you live now and then list every place you lived for the last 5 years.
If you need more space, use a separate sheet of paper.

Street Number and Name, Apartment Number, City, State, Zip Code and Country	Dates *(Month/Year)*	
	From	To
Current Home Address - Same as Part 4.A	_ _/_ _ _ _	Present
	_ _/_ _ _ _	_ _/_ _ _ _
	_ _/_ _ _ _	_ _/_ _ _ _
	_ _/_ _ _ _	_ _/_ _ _ _
	_ _/_ _ _ _	_ _/_ _ _ _

Employment

Listen to Maria

I work at the Holiday Hotel in Dallas, Texas. Holiday Hotel is my employer. I've worked there since 1992.

I'm a housekeeper. This is my only job. I don't have any other jobs. I haven't worked in any other place in the U.S.

Maria's Form

B. Where have you worked (or, if you were a student, what schools did you attend) during the last 5 years? Include military service. Begin with your current or latest employer and then list every place you have worked or studied for the last 5 years. If you need more space, use a separate sheet of paper.

| Employer or School Name | Employer or School Address *(Street, City and State)* | Dates *(Month/Year)* | | Your Occupation |
		From	To	
HOLIDAY HOTEL	125 SPRING ST. DALLAS, TX	0 9 / 1 9 9 2	PRESENT	HOUSE-KEEPER
		_ _ / _ _ _ _	_ _ / _ _ _ _	

What Will Maria Say?

Have you had any other jobs in the last five years?

_____ **a.** No.

_____ **b.** Since 1992.

_____ **c.** Holiday Hotel.

Maria's Interview

EXAMINER: Are you still working at the Holiday Hotel?

MARIA: Yes.

EXAMINER: How long have you worked there?

MARIA: How long? Uh . . . since 1992.

EXAMINER: What do you do there?

MARIA: I'm a housekeeper.

EXAMINER: Have you had any other jobs in the last five years?

MARIA: No.

Listen to Hai

I have my own store. I'm a store manager. My family bought the store in 1998. I am self-employed. I don't have a boss.

Before we bought the store, I worked in Green's Market. I was a cashier. Also, I was a gas station attendant at Springfield Arco.

Hai's Form

B. Where have you worked (or, if you were a student, what schools did you attend) during the last 5 years? Include military service. Begin with your current or latest employer and then list every place you have worked or studied for the last 5 years. If you need more space, use a separate sheet of paper.

Employer or School Name	Employer or School Address (Street, City and State)	Dates (Month/Year)		Your Occupation
		From	To	
SELF-EMPLOYED, ASIAN AMERICAN MARKET	2123 NORTH 16TH ST. OAKLAND, CA	05/1998	PRESENT	MANAGER
GREEN'S MARKET	43 MAIN ST. OAKLAND, CA	12/1995	05/1998	CASHIER
ARCO	515 MAIN ST. OAKLAND, CA	01/1996	03/1997	GAS STATION ATTENDANT
		_ _/_ _ _ _	_ _/_ _ _ _	
		_ _/_ _ _ _	_ _/_ _ _ _	

What Will Hai Say?

Who is your current employer?

_____ **a.** No, I don't.

_____ **b.** We sell food.

_____ **c.** I'm self-employed.

Hai's Interview

EXAMINER: What is your occupation?

HAI: I'm a store manager.

EXAMINER: Who is your current employer?

HAI: I'm self-employed.

EXAMINER: So you work for yourself?

HAI: Yes, that's right. My family owns a store.

EXAMINER: How long have you been managing the store?

HAI: Since 1999. Before that I was a cashier at Green's Market.

EXAMINER: When did you begin that job?

HAI: Let me think. . . . I think that was in 1995.

EXAMINER: Have you worked anywhere else since you came to America?

HAI: Yes. I worked at a gas station for a couple of years.

EXAMINER: What was the name of the gas station?

HAI: Springfield Arco.

EXAMINER: And do you remember the dates that you worked there?

HAI: I'm sorry. It's hard to remember. I think it was around 1997 . . . maybe 1996 also.

Listen to Otto

I'm retired. I don't work anymore. I stopped working nine years ago. Now I stay at home. I also spend a lot of time in the park.

Otto's Form

B. Where have you worked (or, if you were a student, what schools did you attend) during the last 5 years? Include military service.
Begin with your current or latest employer and then list every place you have worked or studied for the last 5 years. If you need more space, use a separate sheet of paper.

Employer or School Name	Employer or School Address (Street, City and State)	Dates (Month/Year)		Your Occupation
		From	To	
RETIRED-N/A		_ _/_ _ _ _	_ _/_ _ _ _	

What Will Otto Say?

Have you been employed in the last five years?

_____ **a.** Yes, I stay home.

_____ **b.** No. I don't work anymore.

_____ **c.** Nine years ago.

Otto's Interview

EXAMINER: Have you been employed in the last five years?

OTTO: Employed?

EXAMINER: Have you worked? Did you have a job?

OTTO: No. I don't work anymore.

EXAMINER: You're retired?

OTTO: Yes. Retired.

EXAMINER: How long have you been retired?

OTTO: Nine years.

Listen to Chong

I just got a job in a restaurant. I'm a waitress.

Before that I didn't work. I went to English classes and I stayed home with my children.

Chong's Form

B. Where have you worked (or, if you were a student, what schools did you attend) during the last 5 years? Include military service.
Begin with your current or latest employer and then list every place you have worked or studied for the last 5 years. If you need more space, use a separate sheet of paper.

Employer or School Name	Employer or School Address *(Street, City and State)*	Dates *(Month/Year)*		Your Occupation
		From	To	
LUCY'S DINER	45 MAPLE ST. EDMONDS, WA	06/2000	PRESENT __/_____	WAITRESS
EDMONDS ADULT EDUCATION	42 MAIN ST. EDMONDS, WA	03/1997	11/1999	STUDENT
		__/_____	__/_____	

What Will Chong Say?

What do you do at Lucy's Diner?

_____ **a.** I'm on welfare.

_____ **b.** I'm a waitress.

_____ **c.** Yes, it's my job.

Chong's Interview

EXAMINER: Are you currently employed?

CHONG: You mean . . . working?

EXAMINER: Yes. Do you have a job?

CHONG: Yes. I work at Lucy's Diner.

EXAMINER: What is your position there?

CHONG: Position?

EXAMINER: Your occupation, your job. What do you do at Lucy's Diner?

CHONG: Oh. I'm a waitress.

EXAMINER: What did you do before that?

CHONG: I didn't have a job. I stayed home to take care of my children. And I went to English classes.

EXAMINER: How did you support yourself?

CHONG: Support?

EXAMINER: How did you get money to pay the rent? Buy food?

CHONG: Oh. I was on welfare. And my husband paid child support.

What Will You Say? 🔊

Do you work?

Do you have a job right now?

Are you currently employed?

Are you currently working?

Who is your current employer?

Where do you work?

What is your employer's address?

How long have you worked there?

When did you begin working there?

How long have you been working there?

How long have you had that job?

What do you do there?

What kind of work do you do?

What is your position?

What job do you have there?

What is your occupation?

Where did you work before that?

What did you do?

When did you leave that job?

How long did you work there?

Have you had any other jobs?

Have you worked anywhere else in the last five years?

Where else have you worked since you became a permanent resident?

Your Form

B. Where have you worked (or, if you were a student, what schools did you attend) during the last 5 years? Include military service. Begin with your current or latest employer and then list every place you have worked or studied for the last 5 years. If you need more space, use a separate sheet of paper.

Employer or School Name	Employer or School Address (Street, City and State)	Dates (Month/Year)		Your Occupation
		From	To	
		— —/— — — —	— —/— — — —	
		— —/— — — —	— — — — — —	
		— —/— — — —	— —/— — — —	
		— —/— — — —	— —/— — — —	
		— —/— — — —	— —/— — — —	

N-400 Part 7
Time outside the United States

Listen to Hai

After I came to America, I stayed here. I did not leave America.

I did not take any trips outside this country.

Hai's Form

> **Part 7. Time Outside the United States**
> *(Including Trips to Canada, Mexico, and the Caribbean Islands)*
>
> A. How many total days did you spend outside of the United States during the past 5 years?   **0** days
>
> B. How many trips of 24 hours or more have you taken outside of the United States during the past 5 years?   **0** trips
>
> C. List below all the trips of 24 hours or more that you have taken outside of the United States since becoming a Lawful Permanent Resident. Begin with your most recent trip. If you need more space, use a separate sheet of paper.

Date You Left the United States (Month/Day/Year)	Date You Returned to the United States (Month/Day/Year)	Did Trip Last 6 Months or More?	Countries to Which You Traveled	Total Days Out of the United States
__/__/____	__/__/____	☐ Yes ☐ No	**N/A**	
__/__/____	__/__/____	☐ Yes ☐ No		

What Will Hai Say?

Have you left the United States since you became a permanent resident?

_____ **a.** July 8, 1993.

_____ **b.** No.

_____ **c.** Yes, Vietnam.

Hai's Interview

EXAMINER: Have you left the United States since you became a permanent resident?

HAI: I'm sorry. I didn't hear. Can you say that again?

EXAMINER: Have you left the U.S.? Have you gone to any other countries?

HAI: Other country? No.

EXAMINER: You haven't visited your family in Vietnam?

HAI: No. I stay here.

Listen to Maria

I go to Mexico every year to see my mother. I stay with her for two weeks. Then I come home.

I can not remember exactly which dates I stayed in Mexico. I wrote the dates I could remember on my form.

Maria's Form

Part 7. Time Outside the United States
(Including Trips to Canada, Mexico, and the Caribbean Islands)

A. How many total days did you spend outside of the United States during the past 5 years? **73?** days

B. How many trips of 24 hours or more have you taken outside of the United States during the past 5 years? **5** trips

C. List below all the trips of 24 hours or more that you have taken outside of the United States since becoming a Lawful Permanent Resident. Begin with your most recent trip. If you need more space, use a separate sheet of paper.

Date You Left the United States (Month/Day/Year)	Date You Returned to the United States (Month/Day/Year)	Did Trip Last 6 Months or More?	Countries to Which You Traveled	Total Days Out of the United States
02/01/1997	02/??/1997	☐ Yes ☑ No	MEXICO	14?
11/??/1998	12/??/1998	☐ Yes ☑ No	MEXICO	14?
03/15/1999	03/30/1999	☐ Yes ☑ No	MEXICO	15
12/02/2000	12/14/2000	☐ Yes ☑ No	MEXICO	12
02/20/2001	03/10/2001	☐ Yes ☑ No	MEXICO	18
__/__/____	__/__/____	☐ Yes ☐ No		

What Will Maria Say?

How long did you stay in Mexico?

_____ **a.** No, I didn't.

_____ **b.** Last year.

_____ **c.** Two weeks.

Maria's Interview

EXAMINER: Have you spent any time outside the U.S. since you became a
                        permanent resident?

MARIA: No . . . ?

EXAMINER: Are you sure?

MARIA: Uh . . . I went to Mexico many times.

EXAMINER: How long did you stay in Mexico?

MARIA: Two weeks. I stay two weeks, then I come back, every year.

Listen to Chong

I have been outside the U.S. one time since I came here.
My family went to Canada for vacation in 1999. We left on
July 14 and we returned on July 29. We were away for
two weeks.

Chong's Form

Part 7. Time Outside the United States
(Including Trips to Canada, Mexico, and the Caribbean Islands)

A. How many total days did you spend outside of the United States during the past 5 years?   **15** days

B. How many trips of 24 hours or more have you taken outside of the United States during the past 5 years?   **1** trips

C. List below all the trips of 24 hours or more that you have taken outside of the United States since becoming a Lawful
   Permanent Resident. Begin with your most recent trip. If you need more space, use a separate sheet of paper.

Date You Left the United States *(Month/Day/Year)*	Date You Returned to the United States *(Month/Day/Year)*	Did Trip Last 6 Months or More?	Countries to Which You Traveled	Total Days Out of the United States
07/14/1999	07/29/1999	☐ Yes ☑ No	CANADA	15
__/__/____	__/__/____	☐ Yes ☐ No		

What Will Chong Say?

How long did you stay in Canada?

_____ **a.** Two weeks.

_____ **b.** For vacation.

_____ **c.** July 14.

Chong's Interview

EXAMINER: Have you been outside the U.S. in the last five years?
CHONG: Yes. One time.
EXAMINER: Where did you go?
CHONG: Canada.
EXAMINER: How long did you stay in Canada?
CHONG: Two weeks.
EXAMINER: Do you remember when that was?
CHONG: Yes. It was in July . . . uh, 1999.

Listen to Sergei

My father died in 1998. I went to Russia for my father's funeral. I stayed from January 12 to February 20.

I went back to Russia another time for my brother's wedding. He got married in June 2000. I stayed from June 1 to June 25.

I was absent from the U.S. two times since I became a permanent resident. Both times I went to Russia.

Sergei's Form

Part 7. Time Outside the United States
(Including Trips to Canada, Mexico, and the Caribbean Islands)

A. How many total days did you spend outside of the United States during the past 5 years? **64** days

B. How many trips of 24 hours or more have you taken outside of the United States during the past 5 years? **2** trips

C. List below all the trips of 24 hours or more that you have taken outside of the United States since becoming a Lawful Permanent Resident. Begin with your most recent trip. If you need more space, use a separate sheet of paper.

Date You Left the United States *(Month/Day/Year)*	Date You Returned to the United States *(Month/Day/Year)*	Did Trip Last 6 Months or More?	Countries to Which You Traveled	Total Days Out of the United States
01/12/1998	02/20/1998	☐ Yes ☑ No	RUSSIA	39
06/01/2000	06/25/2000	☐ Yes ☑ No	RUSSIA	25
__/__/____	__/__/____	☐ Yes ☐ No		

What Will Sergei Say?

Have you taken any trips since 1997?

_____ **a.** No, that's all.

_____ **b.** Yes. Two trips.

_____ **c.** For a wedding.

Sergei's Interview 📻

EXAMINER: It says here that you've made two trips out of the country since you became a permanent resident.

SERGEI: Yes.

EXAMINER: Both to Russia, is that right?

SERGEI: Yes. In 1998 and 2000.

EXAMINER: Have you taken any other trips since 1997?

SERGEI: You mean . . . more trips?

EXAMINER: Yes.

SERGEI: No. No more trips.

What Will You Say? 📻

Have you taken any trips outside the U.S. in the last five years?
Have you left the United States since you came here?
Have you ever left the country?
Have you traveled outside the country in the last five years?

How many times did you go outside the U.S.?
How many trips have you taken outside the U.S.?

When did you leave the U.S.?
When did you return?

How long were you gone?
How many days were you outside the U.S.?
For how long were you away?
How long was your trip?

Did you stay outside of the U.S. for six months?

Where did you go?
Which country did you visit?

Have you been outside the U.S. any other times?
Have you taken any trips since then?
Did you take any other trips outside the U.S.?

Your Form

Part 7. Time Outside the United States
(Including Trips to Canada, Mexico, and the Caribbean Islands)

A. How many total days did you spend outside of the United States during the past 5 years? [   ] days

B. How many trips of 24 hours or more have you taken outside of the United States during the past 5 years? [   ] trips

C. List below all the trips of 24 hours or more that you have taken outside of the United States since becoming a Lawful Permanent Resident. Begin with your most recent trip. If you need more space, use a separate sheet of paper.

Date You Left the United States *(Month/Day/Year)*	Date You Returned to the United States *(Month/Day/Year)*	Did Trip Last 6 Months or More?	Countries to Which You Traveled	Total Days Out of the United States
___/___/_____	___/___/_____	☐ Yes ☐ No		
___/___/_____	___/___/_____	☐ Yes ☐ No		
___/___/_____	___/___/_____	☐ Yes ☐ No		
___/___/_____	___/___/_____	☐ Yes ☐ No		
___/___/_____	___/___/_____	☐ Yes ☐ No		
___/___/_____	___/___/_____	☐ Yes ☐ No		
___/___/_____	___/___/_____	☐ Yes ☐ No		
___/___/_____	___/___/_____	☐ Yes ☐ No		
___/___/_____	___/___/_____	☐ Yes ☐ No		
___/___/_____	___/___/_____	☐ Yes ☐ No		

N-400 Part 8
Information about Your Marital History

Single

Listen to Hai

I'm single. I have never been married. I don't have anything
to write in Part 8.

Hai's Form

> **Part 8. Information About Your Marital History**
>
> A. How many times have you been married (including annulled marriages)? [0] If you have NEVER been married, go to Part 9.
>
> B. If you are now married, give the following information about your spouse:
>
> | 1. Spouse's Family Name *(Last Name)* | Given Name *(First Name)* | Full Middle Name *(If applicable)* |
> |---|---|---|
> | N/A | | |
>
> 2. Date of Birth *(Month/Day/Year)*   3. Date of Marriage *(Month/Day/Year)*   4. Spouse's Social Security Number
> __ __ / __ __ / __ __ __ __   __ __ / __ __ / __ __ __ __   __ __ __ - __ __ - __ __ __ __
>
> 5. Home Address - Street Number and Name   Apartment Number
>
> City   State   ZIP Code

What Will Hai Say?

Have you ever been married before?

_____ **a.** No.

_____ **b.** Yes, single.

_____ **c.** My wife.

Hai's Interview

EXAMINER: Are you married?

HAI: Married? No.

EXAMINER: Have you ever been married before?

HAI: No. Never.

Information about Your Spouse

Listen to Susan

In my life I have had just one husband. My husband's name is Jean Claud Santos.

He was born on March 10, 1976. March 10, 1976, is his date of birth.

We got married on June 12, 1999. June 12, 1999, is our date of marriage.

My husband lives with me. His address and my address are the same.

Susan's Form

Part 8. Information About Your Marital History

A. How many times have you been married (including annulled marriages)? | 1 | If you have NEVER been married, go to Part 9.

B. If you are now married, give the following information about your spouse:

1. Spouse's Family Name *(Last Name)* | Given Name *(First Name)* | Full Middle Name *(If applicable)*

SANTOS | **JEAN** | **CLAUD**

2. Date of Birth *(Month/Day/Year)* | 3. Date of Marriage *(Month/Day/Year)* | 4. Spouse's Social Security Number

03/10/1976 | **06/12/1999** | **124-56-2998**

5. Home Address - Street Number and Name | Apartment Number

WITH ME

City | State | ZIP Code

What Will Susan Say?

You have a husband now, is that right?

_____ **a.** Yes.

_____ **b.** In 1999.

_____ **c.** He's at work now.

Susan's Interview 📻

EXAMINER: How many times have you been married?
SUSAN: I got married in 1999.
EXAMINER: I'm asking you how many times.
SUSAN: I don't understand.
EXAMINER: Did you ever have a different husband before Jean Claud?
SUSAN: No. Jean Claud is the only one.

Listen to Susan 📻

 My husband was born in Haiti, but he's a U.S. citizen now.
He became a citizen on January 16, 1998, in New York City.

Susan's Form

Part 8. Information About Your Marital History *(Continued)*

C. Is your spouse a U.S. citizen?　　☑ Yes　　　☐ No

D. If your spouse is a U.S. citizen, give the following information:

　1. When did your spouse become a U.S. citizen?　　　☐ At Birth　　☑ Other

　　If "Other," give the following information:

2. Date your spouse became a U.S. citizen	3. Place your spouse became a U.S. citizen *(Please see Instructions)*
01/16/1998	NEW YORK, NY
	City and State

What Will Susan Say?

Your husband is a U.S. citizen, is that correct?
_____ **a.** Yes. I want to be a citizen.
_____ **b.** Yes. He is a citizen.
_____ **c.** Yes. I have a husband.

Susan's Interview 📻

EXAMINER: Your husband is a U.S. citizen, is that correct?
SUSAN: Yes. He is a citizen.
EXAMINER: Do you know when he became a citizen? What date was it?
SUSAN: I don't remember the date exactly. But the year was 1998.
EXAMINER: Do you know where he became a citizen?
SUSAN: Um . . . let me see. New York, I think. . . Yes, New York City.

Listen to Nick

 My wife is not a U.S. citizen. She is a permanent resident. She is also from Cambodia, like me.

Nick's Form

E. If your spouse is NOT a U.S. citizen, give the following information :

1. Spouse's Country of Citizenship

CAMBODIA

2. Spouse's USCIS "A"- Number *(If applicable)*

A **223000093**

3. Spouse's Immigration Status

☑ Lawful Permanent Resident   ☐ Other _____

What Will Nick Say?

Is your wife a U.S. citizen?

_____ **a.** I'm married.

_____ **b.** No. She has a green card.

_____ **c.** After three years.

Nick's Interview

EXAMINER: Is your wife a citizen of the United States?

NICK: Excuse me. You ask about my wife, right?

EXAMINER: Yes. Is she a U.S. citizen?

NICK: No. She has a green card.

EXAMINER: So she's a permanent resident.

NICK: Yes.

Listen to Maria

My husband's name was José Maria Perez. We were married on June 16, 1957.

José was a permanent resident. He died August 1, 1997.

Maria's Form

F. If you were married before, provide the following information about your prior spouse. If you have more than one previous marriage, use a separate sheet of paper to provide the information requested in questions 1-5 below.

1. Prior Spouse's Family Name *(Last Name)*   Given Name *(First Name)*   Full Middle Name *(If applicable)*

PEREZ   JOSE   MARIA

2. Prior Spouse's Immigration Status

☐ U.S. Citizen
☑ Lawful Permanent Resident
☐ Other _____

3. Date of Marriage *(Month/Day/Year)*

06/16/1957

4. Date Marriage Ended *(Month/Day/Year)*

08/01/1997

5. How Marriage Ended

☐ Divorce   ☑ Spouse Died   ☐ Other _____

What Will Maria Say?

Was your husband a U.S. citizen?

_____ **a.** No. He died in 1997.

_____ **b.** No. He was a permanent resident.

_____ **c.** Only one time.

Maria's Interview

EXAMINER: How many times have you been married?

MARIA: Only one time.

EXAMINER: And you got married in 1997, right?

MARIA: No, in 1957. 1997 was the year my husband died.

EXAMINER: Was your husband a U.S. citizen?

MARIA: No. He was a permanent resident.

Listen to Susan

My husband was divorced before he married me.

A long time ago he had a different wife, Marianne. Marianne is his former wife. She is his previous wife.

Susan's Form

G. How many times has your current spouse been married (including annulled marriages)? **2**

If your spouse has EVER been married before, give the following information about your spouse's prior marriage.
If your spouse has more than one previous marriage, use a separate sheet of paper to provide the information requested in questions 1 - 5 below.

1. Prior Spouse's Family Name *(Last Name)* **SANTOS**

Given Name *(First Name)* **MARIANNE**

Full Middle Name *(If applicable)* **N/A**

2. Prior Spouse's Immigration Status
- ☐ U.S. Citizen
- ☐ Lawful Permanent Resident
- ☑ Other **CITIZEN OF HAITI**

3. Date of Marriage *(Month/Day/Year)* **11/01/1992**

4. Date Marriage Ended *(Month/Day/Year)* **02/28/1994**

5. How Marriage Ended
- ☑ Divorce ☐ Spouse Died ☐ Other _____

What Will Susan Say?

Do you know the date of your husband's divorce?
_____ **a.** Yes, he is divorced.
_____ **b.** It means not married anymore.
_____ **c.** It was in '94, I think.

Susan's Interview

EXAMINER: Tell me about your husband. Has he ever been married before?
SUSAN: Yes. He got divorced.
EXAMINER: Do you know when that happened?
SUSAN: Excuse me . . . can you ask the question again?
EXAMINER: Do you know the date of your husband's divorce?
SUSAN: I don't remember exactly. In 1994, I guess.
EXAMINER: And his former wife . . . was she a permanent resident?
SUSAN: No. They were married in Haiti. She never lived in America.

What Will You Say? 📻

Are you married?
Are you currently married?
Have you ever been married?
How many times have you been married?

When were you married?
What was the date of your marriage?

Is this your first marriage?
Were you ever married before this?
Have you had any previous marriages?

Questions for a Woman with a Husband or Former Husband

– What's your husband's name?
– What's his date of birth?
– Was he born in the U.S.?

– Does he live with you?
– Where does he live?

– What is his immigration status?
– Is he a U.S. citizen?
– Is he a permanent resident?
– When did he become a citizen?
– Where did he become a citizen?

– How many times has he been married?
– Has he ever been married before this?
– Has he had any previous marriages?
– Does he have a former wife?

– Do you have any former husbands?
– Do you have any prior husbands?

Questions for a Man with a Wife or Former Wife

– What's your wife's name?
– What's her date of birth?
– Was she born in the U.S.?

– Does she live with you?
– Where does she live?

– What is her immigration status?
– Is she a U.S. citizen?
– Is she a permanent resident?
– When did she become a citizen?
– Where did she become a citizen?

– How many times has she been married?
– Has she ever been married before this?
– Has she had any previous marriages?
– Does she have a former husband?

– Do you have any former wives?
– Do you have any previous wives?

Your Form

Part 8. Information About Your Marital History

A. How many times have you been married (including annulled marriages)? [   ] If you have NEVER been married, go to Part 9.

B. If you are now married, give the following information about your spouse:

1. Spouse's Family Name *(Last Name)*   Given Name *(First Name)*   Full Middle Name *(If applicable)*

2. Date of Birth *(Month/Day/Year)*

___/___/____

3. Date of Marriage *(Month/Day/Year)*

___/___/____

4. Spouse's Social Security Number

___ ___ ___ - ___ ___ - ___ ___ ___ ___

5. Home Address - Street Number and Name

Apartment Number

City

State

ZIP Code

C. Is your spouse a U.S. citizen? ☐ Yes ☐ No

D. If your spouse is a U.S. citizen, give the following information:

1. When did your spouse become a U.S. citizen? ☐ At Birth ☐ Other

If "Other," give the following information:

2. Date your spouse became a U.S. citizen

___/___/____

3. Place your spouse became a U.S. citizen *(Please see Instructions)*

City and State

E. If your spouse is NOT a U.S. citizen, give the following information :

1. Spouse's Country of Citizenship

2. Spouse's USCIS "A"- Number *(If applicable)*

A___ ___ ___ ___ ___ ___ ___ ___ ___

3. Spouse's Immigration Status

☐ Lawful Permanent Resident ☐ Other _____

F. If you were married before, provide the following information about your prior spouse. If you have more than one previous marriage, use a separate sheet of paper to provide the information requested in questions 1-5 below.

1. Prior Spouse's Family Name *(Last Name)*

Given Name *(First Name)*

Full Middle Name *(If applicable)*

2. Prior Spouse's Immigration Status

☐ U.S. Citizen

☐ Lawful Permanent Resident

☐ Other _____

3. Date of Marriage *(Month/Day/Year)*

___/___/____

4. Date Marriage Ended *(Month/Day/Year)*

___/___/____

5. How Marriage Ended

☐ Divorce ☐ Spouse Died ☐ Other _____

G. How many times has your current spouse been married (including annulled marriages)?

If your spouse has EVER been married before, give the following information about your spouse's prior marriage.
If your spouse has more than one previous marriage, use a separate sheet of paper to provide the information requested in questions 1 - 5 below.

1. Prior Spouse's Family Name *(Last Name)*

Given Name *(First Name)*

Full Middle Name *(If applicable)*

2. Prior Spouse's Immigration Status

☐ U.S. Citizen

☐ Lawful Permanent Resident

☐ Other _____

3. Date of Marriage *(Month/Day/Year)*

___/___/____

4. Date Marriage Ended *(Month/Day/Year)*

___/___/____

5. How Marriage Ended

☐ Divorce ☐ Spouse Died ☐ Other _____

N-400 Part 9
Information about Your Children

Listen to Hai

I don't have any children. I've never had any children.

Hai's Form

Part 9. Information About Your Children

A. How many sons and daughters have you had? For more information on which sons and daughters you should include and how to complete this section, see the Instructions.

0

B. Provide the following information about all of your sons and daughters. If you need more space, use a separate sheet of paper.

Full Name of Son or Daughter	Date of Birth (Month/Day/Year)	USCIS "A"- number (if child has one)	Country of Birth	Current Address (Street, City, State & Country)
N/A	__/__/____	A_____		
	__/__/____	A_____		

What Will Hai Say?

You don't have any children, do you?

_____ **a.** Yes.

_____ **b.** No.

_____ **c.** My family.

Hai's Interview

EXAMINER: You don't have any children, do you?

HAI: No. No children.

Listen to Chong

I have two children, Amy and Tom. My daughter Amy was born in Korea in 1989. Korea is her country of birth.

My son Tom was born in the U.S. Tom is a U.S. citizen. He doesn't have an "A" number.

My children live with me.

Chong's Form

Part 9. Information About Your Children

A. How many sons and daughters have you had? For more information on which sons and daughters you should include and how to complete this section, see the Instructions.

2

B. Provide the following information about all of your sons and daughters. If you need more space, use a separate sheet of paper.

Full Name of Son or Daughter	Date of Birth (Month/Day/Year)	USCIS "A"- number (if child has one)	Country of Birth	Current Address (Street, City, State & Country)
AMY BARTON	01/14/1989	A 134332889	KOREA	WITH ME
TOM BARTON	04/08/1991	A N/A	U.S.A.	WITH ME
	__/__/____	A _____		

What Will Chong Say?

Where do your children live? Are they both with you?

_____ **a.** Yes, with me.

_____ **b.** No, one was born in Korea.

_____ **c.** My children are citizens.

Chong's Interview

EXAMINER: How many children do you have?

CHONG: Two.

EXAMINER: And they were born in the United States?

CHONG: My daughter was born in Korea. My son was born in the United States.

EXAMINER: And where do your children live? Are they both with you?

CHONG: Yes, with me.

Listen to Maria

I've had three children in my life. They were all born in Mexico.

My son Juan Carlos came to America first. He became a U.S. citizen. He helped us to come to America. He lives in Los Angeles now.

I lost my second son, Oscar, in 1985. He died in an accident. He is dead.

I don't know where my son José is. I have not seen him in 15 years. I don't know his address. He is missing.

Maria's Form

Part 9. Information About Your Children				

A. How many sons and daughters have you had? For more information on which sons and daughters you should include and how to complete this section, see the Instructions.   **3**

B. Provide the following information about all of your sons and daughters. If you need more space, use a separate sheet of paper.

Full Name of Son or Daughter	Date of Birth (Month/Day/Year)	USCIS "A"- number (if child has one)	Country of Birth	Current Address (Street, City, State & Country)
JUAN CARLOS PEREZ	04/09/1962	A___N/A_____	MEXICO	1213 ROOSEVELT BLVD. LOS ANGELES, CA, USA
OSCAR PEREZ	06/17/1964	A___N/A_____	MEXICO	DEAD
JOSE PEREZ	12/24/1971	A___N/A_____	MEXICO	MISSING
	__/__/____	A_____		

What Will Maria Say?

Were your children born in Mexico?

_____ **a.** I don't know.

_____ **b.** Yes.

_____ **c.** They are missing.

Maria's Interview 📻

EXAMINER: You have three children, is that correct?

MARIA: No. One died. Now I have only two children.

EXAMINER: Oh. I'm sorry to hear that. So you have two living children.

MARIA: Yes.

EXAMINER: And were your children born in Mexico?

MARIA: Yes.

EXAMINER: Where do they live now?

MARIA: Juan Carlos lives in Los Angeles, and I . . . José . . . I don't know where he is.

What Will You Say? 📻

Do you have any children?
Do you have any sons or daughters?
How many children do you have?

What are their names?

What are their dates of birth?
When were they born?
What are their birth dates?

Where were they born?
In which countries were they born?

Do they live with you?
Where do they live?

Your Form

Part 9. Information About Your Children				

A. How many sons and daughters have you had? For more information on which sons and daughters you should include and how to complete this section, see the Instructions.

B. Provide the following information about all of your sons and daughters. If you need more space, use a separate sheet of paper.

Full Name of Son or Daughter	Date of Birth (Month/Day/Year)	USCIS "A"- number (if child has one)	Country of Birth	Current Address (Street, City, State & Country)
	_ _ / _ _ / _ _ _ _	A_ _ _ _ _ _ _ _ _		
	_ _ / _ _ / _ _ _ _	A_ _ _ _ _ _ _ _ _		
	_ _ / _ _ / _ _ _ _	A_ _ _ _ _ _ _ _ _		
	_ _ / _ _ / _ _ _ _	A_ _ _ _ _ _ _ _ _		
	_ _ / _ _ / _ _ _ _	A_ _ _ _ _ _ _ _ _		
	_ _ / _ _ / _ _ _ _	A_ _ _ _ _ _ _ _ _		
	_ _ / _ _ / _ _ _ _	A_ _ _ _ _ _ _ _ _		
	_ _ / _ _ / _ _ _ _	A_ _ _ _ _ _ _ _ _		

N-400 Part 10
Additional Questions

General Questions

Listen to the USCIS Examiner

Some people cannot be U.S. citizens because of things they did in the past. Here are some examples.

Claiming to Be a U.S. Citizen

Ruth is a permanent resident. She is not a citizen. Six years ago, Ruth wanted a government job. The job was for U.S. citizens only. She wrote, "I am a U.S. citizen." She told the boss, "I am a U.S. citizen."

Ruth **claimed** to be a citizen. She did not tell the truth.

Maybe Ruth cannot become a citizen now. She needs to talk to a lawyer.

Registering to Vote

Joseph is a permanent resident. He is not a citizen. Five years ago, Joseph **registered** to vote. He **voted** in a U.S. election.

Maybe Joseph cannot become a citizen now. He needs to talk to a lawyer.

What about You?

Did you ever lie about being a U.S. citizen?

Did you ever register to vote in the U.S.?
Did you ever vote in a U.S. election?

Your Form

1. Have you **EVER** claimed to be a U.S. citizen *(in writing or any other way)*?	☐ Yes	☐ No
2. Have you **EVER** registered to vote in any Federal, state, or local election in the United States?	☐ Yes	☐ No
3. Have you **EVER** voted in any Federal, state, or local election in the United States?	☐ Yes	☐ No

Failure to Pay Taxes

Jong works in a restaurant. She does not get a paycheck. Her boss pays her cash.

Jong does not pay income tax. She does not **file income tax returns.** She failed to file tax returns.

Before she can be a citizen, Jong needs to pay her taxes. She must pay local, state, and federal taxes for each year she worked.

Title of Nobility

George Harris has a special **title**. He is like a king or a prince. In George's country, people do not call him Mr. Harris. They call him Sir George.

George needs to get rid of his title before he can become a citizen.

What about You?

Do you work?
Do you pay state and federal income taxes every year?
Did you file income tax returns for each year you worked?
Have you paid all the taxes you owe?

Do people in your country call you by a special title?
Do you have a title of nobility in your native country?

4. Since becoming a Lawful Permanent Resident, have you **EVER** failed to file a required Federal, state, or local tax return?	☐ Yes	☐ No
5. Do you owe any Federal, state, or local taxes that are overdue?	☐ Yes	☐ No
6. Do you have any title of nobility in any foreign country?	☐ Yes	☐ No

Mentally Ill 🔊

Karen is mentally ill. She does not understand what is happening around her. She is in a mental hospital.

Karen cannot become a citizen now. She is **legally incompetent**. Maybe someday she will understand what is happening. Then maybe she will become a citizen.

What about You? 🔊

Did you ever stay in a mental hospital?
Did a doctor and judge decide that you could not understand what was happening?
Did another person make decisions for you and sign papers for you?

Your Form

7. Have you ever been declared legally incompetent or been confined to a mental institution within the last 5 years? ☐ Yes   ☐ No

Listen to Hai

I am not a citizen yet. I have not told anyone that I am a citizen.

I have not registered to vote in U.S. elections. I never voted in a U.S. election.

I file income taxes every year. I do not have a title from my country.

I understand what is happening around me.

Hai's Form

Part 10. Additional Questions

Please answer questions 1 through 14. If you answer "Yes" to any of these questions, include a written explanation with this form. Your written explanation should (1) explain why your answer was "Yes," and (2) provide any additional information that helps to explain your answer.

A. General Questions

1. Have you **EVER** claimed to be a U.S. citizen *(in writing or any other way)*? ☐ Yes ☑ No

2. Have you **EVER** registered to vote in any Federal, state, or local election in the United States? ☐ Yes ☑ No

3. Have you **EVER** voted in any Federal, state, or local election in the United States? ☐ Yes ☑ No

4. Since becoming a Lawful Permanent Resident, have you **EVER** failed to file a required Federal, state, or local tax return? ☐ Yes ☑ No

5. Do you owe any Federal, state, or local taxes that are overdue? ☐ Yes ☑ No

6. Do you have any title of nobility in any foreign country? ☐ Yes ☑ No

7. Have you ever been declared legally incompetent or been confined to a mental institution within the last 5 years? ☐ Yes ☑ No

What Will Hai Say?

Have you ever failed to file local, state, or U.S. income taxes?

_____ **a.** Yes.

_____ **b.** Federal tax returns.

_____ **c.** I pay my taxes every year.

Hai's Interview

EXAMINER: Have you ever claimed to be a citizen?

HAI: Claimed? You mean did I lie about it?

EXAMINER: Right.

HAI: No. I tell the truth.

EXAMINER: Have you ever registered to vote or voted in a U.S. election?

HAI: No.

EXAMINER: Have you ever failed to file local, state, or U.S. income taxes?

HAI: I pay my taxes every year.

EXAMINER: Do you owe any overdue taxes?

HAI: I don't understand "overdue."

EXAMINER: Have you paid all of your taxes or is there still some money you haven't paid yet?

HAI: No. I paid everything.

EXAMINER: OK. Do you have a title of nobility from another country—a special name like a king or a prince?

HAI: No.

EXAMINER: Have you ever been declared legally incompetent?

HAI: No.

EXAMINER: What does "legally incompetent" mean?

HAI: It means your mind is not OK. Mental illness.

EXAMINER: That's right.

Affiliations

Listen to Maria 📻

I've been a member of the Faith Church since 1987. I also belong to the Hotel Workers' Union at my job. In Mexico, I was a member of an organization called MPDH.

Maria's Form

B. Affiliations

8. a. Have you **EVER** been a member of or associated with any organization, association, fund, foundation, party, club, society, or similar group in the United States or in any other place? ☑ Yes ☐ No

   b. If you answered "Yes," list the name of each group below. If you need more space, attach the names of the other group(s) o n a separate sheet of paper.

Name of Group	Name of Group
1. FAITH CHURCH	6.
2. UNITED HOTEL WORKERS' UNION LOCAL 21	7.
3. MUJERES PARA DERECHOS HUMANOS	8.
4.	9.
5.	10.

What Will Maria Say?

Are you a member of any organizations?

_____ **a.** Yes. Faith Church in Dallas.

_____ **b.** Yes, I have a job.

_____ **c.** I don't know any members.

Maria's Interview 📻

EXAMINER: Are you a member of any organizations?

MARIA: Could you say that again?

EXAMINER: Are you a member of any organizations?

MARIA: I'm not sure.

EXAMINER: For example, a club or an association?

MARIA: Like my church?

EXAMINER: Yes, that's an organization. So you're a member of a church?

MARIA: Yes, Faith Church in Dallas . . . and, uh . . . let's see . . . I have a union card.

EXAMINER: You're a union member?

MARIA: Yes, United Hotel Workers Union, Local 21.

EXAMINER: What about in your country?

MARIA: In Mexico? Yes. I belonged to a group for mothers of prisoners, called Mujeres Para Derechos Humanos.

What Will You Say? 📻

Do you belong to any groups?

Do you belong to a church or a union?

Do you belong to a club or an organization?

Have you ever belonged to any groups in the U.S.?

Were you a member of any groups in your country?

Your Form

B. Affiliations

8. a. Have you **EVER** been a member of or associated with any organization, association, fund, foundation, party, club, society, or similar group in the United States or in any other place? ☐ Yes ☐ No

b. If you answered "Yes," list the name of each group below. If you need more space, attach the names of the other group(s) o n a separate sheet of paper.

Name of Group	Name of Group
1.	6.
2.	7.
3.	8.
4.	9.
5.	10.

Listen to the INS Examiner

Some people belong to groups that do not agree with the United States. Some people belong to groups that the U.S. does not agree with. Some people belong to groups that want to hurt the United States. Some people think that it's OK to hurt other people.

A person who does these things cannot become a U.S. citizen. Here are some examples.

Communist

Li Xian was a member of the **Communist Party** in her country. She believes in Communism.

Probably Li Xian cannot be a citizen.

Totalitarian Party

Many years ago in Spain, Juan was a leader in a **totalitarian** group. This group hurt and killed people who did not agree with them. They put many people in jail for trying to stop them.

Probably Juan cannot be a citizen.

What about You?

Have you ever been a member of the Communist Party?

Have you ever been a member of a totalitarian party?

Your Form

9. Have you **EVER** been a member of or in any way associated *(either directly or indirectly)* with:		
a. The Communist Party?	☐ Yes	☐ No
b. Any other totalitarian party?	☐ Yes	☐ No
c. A terrorist organization?	☐ Yes	☐ No

Terrorist Organization

Chuck belongs to a group that does not like the United States. His group put a bomb in a building. The bomb killed many people.

Chuck is a member of a **terrorist** organization. This group wants a different government. They plan to fight a war with the United States. They want to fight with guns and bombs. They want to overthrow the U.S. government by force.

Chuck cannot become a U.S. citizen.

Persecuted People

Herman belonged to a group of white men in South Africa. His group did not like black people. He hurt people who were different from him. Herman **persecuted** people.

Probably Herman cannot become a U.S. citizen.

What about You?

Are you a member of a terrorist organization?
Have you ever been a member of a terrorist organization?

Do you want to fight a war against the government of the United States?
Have you ever told people that they should fight a war against the U.S. government?
Have you ever told people that they should fight a war against another country?

Did you ever hurt anyone because
– they looked different from you?
– they belonged to a different religion?
– they came from a different place?

Your Form

9. Have you **EVER** been a member of or in any way associated *(either directly or indirectly)* with:

   a. The Communist Party?   ☐ Yes   ☐ No

   b. Any other totalitarian party?   ☐ Yes   ☐ No

   c. A terrorist organization?   ☐ Yes   ☐ No

10. Have you **EVER** advocated *(either directly or indirectly)* the overthrow of any government by force or violence?   ☐ Yes   ☐ No

11. Have you **EVER** persecuted *(either directly or indirectly)* any person because of race, religion, national origin, membership in a particular social group, or political opinion?   ☐ Yes   ☐ No

Nazi Government

Hans was a **Nazi** in Germany during World War II.

Hans cannot become a U.S. citizen.

What about You?

Did you work for the Nazi government of Germany between 1933 and 1945?

Did you help the Nazi government in World War II?

Your Form

12. Between March 23, 1933, and May 8, 1945, did you work for or associate in any way *(either directly or indirectly)* with:

   a. The Nazi government of Germany?   ☐ Yes   ☐ No

   b. Any government in any area (1) occupied by, (2) allied with, or (3) established with the help of the Nazi government of Germany?   ☐ Yes   ☐ No

   c. Any German, Nazi, or S.S. military unit, paramilitary unit, self-defense unit, vigilante unit, citizen unit, police unit, government agency or office, extermination camp, concentration camp, prisoner of war camp, prison, labor camp, or transit camp?   ☐ Yes   ☐ No

Listen to Sergei

I was a doctor in the Soviet Union. I did not want to join the Communist Party. But only party members could work in my hospital. For doctors, joining the Communist Party was **compulsory.**

I was not a member of any other groups in Russia. I am not a member of any groups in the U.S. either.

Sergei's Form

B. Affiliations

8. a. Have you **EVER** been a member of or associated with any organization, association, fund, foundation, party, club, society, or similar group in the United States or in any other place? ☑ Yes ☐ No

   b. If you answered "Yes," list the name of each group below. If you need more space, attach the names of the other group(s) o n a separate sheet of paper.

Name of Group	Name of Group
1. *SOVIET COMMUNIST PARTY (COMPULSORY)*	6.
2.	7.
3.	8.
4.	9.
5.	10.

9. Have you **EVER** been a member of or in any way associated *(either directly or indirectly)* with:

   a. The Communist Party? ☑ Yes ☐ No

   b. Any other totalitarian party? ☐ Yes ☑ No

   c. A terrorist organization? ☐ Yes ☑ No

10. Have you **EVER** advocated *(either directly or indirectly)* the overthrow of any government by force or violence? ☐ Yes ☑ No

11. Have you **EVER** persecuted *(either directly or indirectly)* any person because of race, religion, national origin, membership in a particular social group, or political opinion? ☐ Yes ☑ No

12. Between March 23, 1933, and May 8, 1945, did you work for or associate in any way *(either directly or indirectly)* with:

   a. The Nazi government of Germany? ☐ Yes ☑ No

   b. Any government in any area (1) occupied by, (2) allied with, or (3) established with the help of the Nazi government of Germany? ☐ Yes ☑ No

   c. Any German, Nazi, or S.S. military unit, paramilitary unit, self-defense unit, vigilante unit, citizen unit, police unit, government agency or office, extermination camp, concentration camp, prisoner of war camp, prison, labor camp, or transit camp? ☐ Yes ☑ No

What Will Sergei Say?

When was that?

_____ **a.** From 1959 to 1987.

_____ **b.** Russia.

_____ **c.** 18 years.

Sergei's Interview 📻

EXAMINER: Have you ever been a member of any organizations?

SERGEI: In the U.S. or in my old country?

EXAMINER: Both.

SERGEI: I was a Communist Party member for my job in Russia. It was compulsory.

EXAMINER: When was that?

SERGEI: From 1959 to 1987. I have an affidavit—a letter—to explain this.

EXAMINER: Did you belong to any other organizations?

SERGEI: No.

EXAMINER: Were you ever a member of the Nazi government of Germany?

SERGEI: No.

EXAMINER: Have you ever persecuted any person because of race, religion, or national origin?

SERGEI: No.

EXAMINER: What does "persecute" mean?

SERGEI: Hurt someone . . . someone different from you.

Residence and Taxes

Listen to the USCIS Examiner 📻

Some people cannot become citizens because they did not tell the truth on their taxes. Here is an example.

Claiming to be a Nonresident 📻

Henry is a permanent resident. But at income tax time, he does not tell the truth. He says, "I am not a U.S. resident. I am a **nonresident**. I do not need to pay taxes."

Probably Henry cannot become a U.S. citizen.

What about You? 📻

Did you ever file tax returns as a nonresident?

Do you say "I am a nonresident" because you don't want to pay taxes?

Did you ever fail to pay taxes because you called yourself a nonresident?

Your Form

C. Continuous Residence

Since becoming a Lawful Permanent Resident of the United States:

13. Have you **EVER** called yourself a "nonresident" on a Federal, state, or local tax return? ☐ Yes ☐ No

14. Have you **EVER** failed to file a Federal, state, or local tax return because you considered yourself to be a "nonresident"? ☐ Yes ☐ No

Good Moral Character

Listen to the USCIS Examiner

 If you have had any problem with the police, you must tell USCIS. If you have been to court for any problems, you must tell USCIS. If you had any problems with the law, it is a good idea to talk to a lawyer before you apply for citizenship

– even if it happened a long time ago
– even if it was not your fault
– even if you think it is not on your record
– even if it happened when you were a child

After taking your fingerprints, USCIS will find out about any problems. Even old problems. Even small problems.

Be careful when you answer these questions.

At your interview, you must tell the truth about what happened.

Listen to Ahmed

 Thirty years ago the police **arrested** me. I was arrested because of a fight. The police said that I hit a man. I was charged with assault. Assault is a **crime**. It's against the law.

The judge did not send me to jail. She put me on parole.

After that, for 30 years, I never had problems with police. When I filled out my application, I did not think a problem from a long time ago was important. Question 16 asks, "Have you ever been arrested?" I checked No on question 16.

I did not tell the truth.

Ahmed's Interview

EXAMINER: Have you ever committed a crime?

AHMED: No.

EXAMINER: Are you sure? You've never been arrested?

AHMED: No.

EXAMINER: I have a report from the FBI. It says that you were arrested in New York for assault in 1975. Do you know anything about that?

AHMED: Well, yes. I was arrested, but it was a mistake.

EXAMINER: On your application you wrote that you have never been arrested. Is that true or a mistake?

AHMED: I don't know. I was arrested, but I never went to jail. That's why I didn't write anything on my application about it.

EXAMINER: I know it was a long time ago, and maybe it was not very serious. But you did not tell the truth. This is a very serious problem for your application.

Listen to Maria

Four years ago, a police officer stopped my car. He said that my car needed a new inspection sticker. I had to pay a fine and get a new inspection sticker. I have not had any other problems with the police.

Maria's Form

D. Good Moral Character

For the purposes of this application, you must answer "Yes" to the following questions, if applicable, even if your records were sealed or otherwise cleared or if anyone, including a judge, law enforcement officer, or attorney, told you that you no longer have a record.

15. Have you **EVER** committed a crime or offense for which you were NOT arrested? ☐ Yes ☑ No

16. Have you **EVER** been arrested, cited, or detained by any law enforcement officer (including INS and military officers) for any reason? ☑ Yes ☐ No

17. Have you **EVER** been charged with committing any crime or offense? ☐ Yes ☑ No

18. Have you **EVER** been convicted of a crime or offense? ☐ Yes ☑ No

19. Have you **EVER** been placed in an alternative sentencing or a rehabilitative program (for example: diversion, deferred prosecution, withheld adjudication, deferred adjudication)? ☐ Yes ☑ No

20. Have you **EVER** received a suspended sentence, been placed on probation, or been paroled? ☐ Yes ☑ No

21. Have you **EVER** been in jail or prison? ☐ Yes ☑ No

If you answered "Yes" to any of questions 15 through 21, complete the following table. If you need more space, use a separate sheet of paper to give the same information.

Why were you arrested, cited, detained, or charged?	Date arrested, cited, detained, or charged (Month/Day/Year)	Where were you arrested, cited, detained or charged? (City, State, Country)	Outcome or disposition of the arrest, citation, detention or charge (No charges filed, charges dismissed, jail, probation, etc.)
EXPIRED CAR INSPECTION STICKER	02/09/1998	DALLAS, TX, USA	NO CHARGES FILED

What Will Maria Say?

Have you ever been in jail?

_____ **a.** I paid a fine.

_____ **b.** Prison.

_____ **c.** No.

Maria's Interview

EXAMINER: Have you ever committed a crime?

MARIA: Crime?

EXAMINER: Have you ever done anything illegal—anything that was against the law?

MARIA: No.

EXAMINER: Have you ever been arrested, cited, or detained by the police?

MARIA: What is "detained"?

EXAMINER: Have you ever been in jail?

MARIA: No. But once I had to pay a fine because of my inspection sticker.

EXAMINER: Have you ever been to court? Did a judge say that something you did was not OK?

MARIA: No.

What Will You Say?

Did you ever break the law?

Have you ever committed a crime?

Have you ever been arrested?

Have you ever had a problem with the police?

Have you ever been to court?

Have you ever been charged or convicted of a crime?

Have you ever been on parole?

Have you ever been in jail?

Your Form

D. Good Moral Character

For the purposes of this application, you must answer "Yes" to the following questions, if applicable, even if your records were sealed or otherwise cleared or if anyone, including a judge, law enforcement officer, or attorney, told you that you no longer have a record.

15. Have you **EVER** committed a crime or offense for which you were NOT arrested? ☐ Yes ☐ No

16. Have you **EVER** been arrested, cited, or detained by any law enforcement officer (including INS and military officers) for any reason? ☐ Yes ☐ No

17. Have you **EVER** been charged with committing any crime or offense? ☐ Yes ☐ No

18. Have you **EVER** been convicted of a crime or offense? ☐ Yes ☐ No

19. Have you **EVER** been placed in an alternative sentencing or a rehabilitative program (for example: diversion, deferred prosecution, withheld adjudication, deferred adjudication)? ☐ Yes ☐ No

20. Have you **EVER** received a suspended sentence, been placed on probation, or been paroled? ☐ Yes ☐ No

21. Have you **EVER** been in jail or prison? ☐ Yes ☐ No

If you answered "Yes" to any of questions 15 through 21, complete the following table. If you need more space, use a separate sheet of paper to give the same information.

Why were you arrested, cited, detained, or charged?	Date arrested, cited, detained, or charged *(Month/Day/Year)*	Where were you arrested, cited, detained or charged? *(City, State, Country)*	Outcome or disposition of the arrest, citation, detention or charge *(No charges filed, charges dismissed, jail, probation, etc.)*

Answer questions 22 through 33. If you answer "Yes" to any of these questions, attach (1) your written explanation why your answer was "Yes," and (2) any additional information or documentation that helps explain your answer.

22. Have you **EVER**:

  a. been a habitual drunkard? ☐ Yes ☐ No

  b. been a prostitute, or procured anyone for prostitution? ☐ Yes ☐ No

  c. sold or smuggled controlled substances, illegal drugs or narcotics? ☐ Yes ☐ No

  d. been married to more than one person at the same time? ☐ Yes ☐ No

  e. helped anyone enter or try to enter the United States illegally? ☐ Yes ☐ No

  f. gambled illegally or received income from illegal gambling? ☐ Yes ☐ No

  g. failed to support your dependents or to pay alimony? ☐ Yes ☐ No

23. Have you **EVER** given false or misleading information to any U.S. government official while applying for any immigration benefit or to prevent deportation, exclusion, or removal? ☐ Yes ☐ No

24. Have you **EVER** lied to any U.S. government official to gain entry or admission into the United States? ☐ Yes ☐ No

Habitual Drunkard

Albert drinks a lot of alcohol. He is **drunk** every day.

Probably Albert cannot become a citizen.

Prostitute

Estela is a **prostitute.**

Men pay her money to sleep with them.

Probably Estela cannot become a citizen.

The men who have sex with Estela probably cannot become citizens either.

What about You?

Do you get drunk every day?
Do you drink too much alcohol?
Have you ever had problems with drinking?

Did you ever get paid for having sex?
Did you ever pay someone to sleep with you?
Did you ever buy or sell sex?

Your Form

22. Have you **EVER:**

   a. been a habitual drunkard? ☐ Yes ☐ No

   b. been a prostitute, or procured anyone for prostitution? ☐ Yes ☐ No

   c. sold or smuggled controlled substances, illegal drugs or narcotics? ☐ Yes ☐ No

   d. been married to more than one person at the same time? ☐ Yes ☐ No

   e. helped anyone enter or try to enter the United States illegally? ☐ Yes ☐ No

   f. gambled illegally or received income from illegal gambling? ☐ Yes ☐ No

   g. failed to support your dependents or to pay alimony? ☐ Yes ☐ No

Controlled Substances

Tu sells **illegal drugs** like marijuana, cocaine, and heroin.

Tu cannot become a citizen.

Married to More Than One Person

Chimme has two wives. This is OK in his country. It's not OK in the U.S.

He cannot become a citizen.

What about You?

Do you sell drugs?
Did you ever sell drugs?
Have you ever had any problems with marijuana or cocaine?
Did you ever bring illegal drugs into this country?

Do you have more than one husband or wife?

Your Form

22. Have you **EVER:**

   a. been a habitual drunkard? ☐ Yes ☐ No

   b. been a prostitute, or procured anyone for prostitution? ☐ Yes ☐ No

   c. sold or smuggled controlled substances, illegal drugs or narcotics? ☐ Yes ☐ No

   d. been married to more than one person at the same time? ☐ Yes ☐ No

   e. helped anyone enter or try to enter the United States illegally? ☐ Yes ☐ No

   f. gambled illegally or received income from illegal gambling? ☐ Yes ☐ No

   g. failed to support your dependents or to pay alimony? ☐ Yes ☐ No

Helped Anyone Enter the U.S. Illegally

Manuel helps people come to the U.S. These people do not have green cards. They do not have visas. They pay Manuel a lot of money. He helps them **enter the U.S. illegally**.

Manuel cannot become a citizen.

Gambled Illegally

Sin likes to play cards. He wants to win a lot of money. He does not play in a casino. He plays in secret. He plays where the police cannot see him. Sin likes **gambling**.

Probably Sin cannot become a citizen.

What about You?

Did you ever help someone come to the U.S. without a visa?
Did you ever help anyone enter the U.S. illegally?

Do you play cards for money?
Do you play in secret?
Did you ever take money from illegal gambling?

Your Form

22. Have you **EVER:**

   a. been a habitual drunkard? ☐ Yes ☐ No

   b. been a prostitute, or procured anyone for prostitution? ☐ Yes ☐ No

   c. sold or smuggled controlled substances, illegal drugs or narcotics? ☐ Yes ☐ No

   d. been married to more than one person at the same time? ☐ Yes ☐ No

   e. helped anyone enter or try to enter the United States illegally? ☐ Yes ☐ No

   f. gambled illegally or received income from illegal gambling? ☐ Yes ☐ No

   g. failed to support your dependents or to pay alimony? ☐ Yes ☐ No

Failed to Support Dependents

Raul left his wife and children. He does not send them any money. He does not support his dependents. He does not pay his wife any money. He has failed to pay **alimony** or child **support**.

False or Misleading Information

Boris wanted to come to America. But he didn't get a visa. He found a woman with a green card. He paid the woman to say that she was his mother. He used papers that were not real. He came to America and got a green card.

He did not tell the truth. He **lied** to USCIS. Boris cannot be a citizen.

What about You?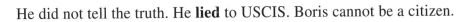

Do your children live with you?
Do you support your children?
Are you required to make child support payments?
Have you ever failed to pay alimony?
Have you ever failed to support your family?

Did you ever tell USCIS something that was not true?
Did you write anything on your USCIS forms that was not true?
Did you lie to get your green card? Did you lie to get a visa?
Did you lie to USCIS so that you could stay in the U.S.?

Your Form

22. Have you **EVER**:

    a. been a habitual drunkard?   ☐ Yes   ☐ No

    b. been a prostitute, or procured anyone for prostitution?   ☐ Yes   ☐ No

    c. sold or smuggled controlled substances, illegal drugs or narcotics?   ☐ Yes   ☐ No

    d. been married to more than one person at the same time?   ☐ Yes   ☐ No

    e. helped anyone enter or try to enter the United States illegally?   ☐ Yes   ☐ No

    f. gambled illegally or received income from illegal gambling?   ☐ Yes   ☐ No

    g. failed to support your dependents or to pay alimony?   ☐ Yes   ☐ No

23. Have you **EVER** given false or misleading information to any U.S. government official while applying for any immigration benefit or to prevent deportation, exclusion, or removal?   ☐ Yes   ☐ No

24. Have you **EVER** lied to any U.S. government official to gain entry or admission into the United States?   ☐ Yes   ☐ No

Removal and Deportation

Ordered Deported

Ten years ago, Julio was **deported**. A judge said "You must go back to your country. You cannot stay in the United States."

Probably Julio cannot become a citizen. He should talk to a lawyer.

What about You?

Did USCIS ever tell you that you must go back to your country?
Did a judge order you to leave the U.S.?

Your Form

E. Removal, Exclusion, and Deportation Proceedings

25. Are removal, exclusion, rescission or deportation proceedings pending against you? ☐ Yes ☐ No

26. Have you **EVER** been removed, excluded, or deported from the United States? ☐ Yes ☐ No

27. Have you **EVER** been ordered to be removed, excluded, or deported from the United States? ☐ Yes ☐ No

28. Have you **EVER** applied for any kind of relief from removal, exclusion, or deportation? ☐ Yes ☐ No

Military Service

Deserted from U.S. Armed Forces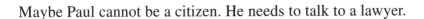

When Paul was young, he was a soldier in the U.S. Army. He served in the Armed Forces.

Paul did not like being in the army. He ran away. He **deserted** from the U.S. Armed Forces.

Maybe Paul cannot be a citizen. He needs to talk to a lawyer.

What about You?

Have you ever served in the U.S. Armed Forces?
Have you ever left the U.S. so that you would not have to serve in the Armed Forces?
Have you ever told the government that you could not serve in the Armed Forces?
If you were a soldier, did you ever desert from the Armed Forces?

Your Form

F. Military Service

	Yes	No
29. Have you **EVER** served in the U.S. Armed Forces?	☐ Yes	☐ No
30. Have you **EVER** left the United States to avoid being drafted into the U.S. Armed Forces?	☐ Yes	☐ No
31. Have you **EVER** applied for any kind of exemption from military service in the U.S. Armed Forces?	☐ Yes	☐ No
32. Have you **EVER** deserted from the U.S. Armed Forces?	☐ Yes	☐ No

Selective Service Registration

Did Not Register with Selective Service System

In America, all men must register for **Selective Service** when they are 18 years old. Every man must be registered until he is 26 years old. Most men register at the Post Office.

Hai came to the U.S. when he was 24. He did not know about the Selective Service law. He did not register.

Hai needs to explain this to USCIS. He needs to tell why he did not register.

What about You?

If you are a man
– Are you between the ages of 18 and 26?
– Were you a resident of the U.S. when you were between the ages of 18 and 26?
– If you answered Yes, did you register for Selective Service?

Your Form

G. Selective Service Registration

33. Are you a male who lived in the United States at any time between your 18th and 26th birthdays in any status except as a lawful nonimmigrant?   ☐ Yes ☐ No

If you answered "NO", go on to question 34.

If you answered "YES", provide the information below.

If you answered "YES", but you did NOT register with the Selective Service System and are still under 26 years of age, you must register before you apply for naturalization, so that you can complete the information below:

Date Registered (Month/Day/Year) [   ]   Selective Service Number [_ _ / _ _ _ _ / _ _ _ _ _]

If you answered "YES", but you did NOT register with the Selective Service and you are now 26 years old or older, attach a statement explaining why you did not register.

Oath Requirements

Listen to Maria

I believe in the government of the United States. I agree with the form of government America has. I believe in the Constitution. I agree with the laws of this country.

I am ready to take the Oath of Allegiance to the United States.

What Will Maria Say?

Do you support the Constitution and form of government of the United States?

_____ **a.** I love my country.

_____ **b.** No, I don't.

_____ **c.** Yes, I do.

What about You?

Do you agree with the form of government of the United States?

Do you agree with the Constitution of the United States?

Do you support the Constitution and form of government of the U.S.?

Your Form

34. Do you support the Constitution and form of government of the United States?	☐ Yes	☐ No

Listen to the CIS Examiner

The Oath of Allegiance is a promise that you make when you become a citizen. The words are old and difficult to understand—even for people who speak English very well.

Listen to the oath. I will explain each part.

OATH: **I hereby declare, on oath . . .**
MEANING: I promise today.

OATH: **. . . that I absolutely and entirely renounce and abjure all allegiance and fidelity to any foreign prince, potentate, state, or sovereignty, of whom or which I have heretofore been a subject or citizen . . .**
MEANING: I am not a citizen of my old country any more. I am a citizen of the U.S. now.

OATH: **. . . that I will support and defend the Constitution and laws of the United States of America . . .**
MEANING: I believe in the Constitution and the laws of the United States, and I will support them.

OATH: **. . . against all enemies, foreign and domestic . . .**
MEANING: I will not let anyone—from this country or from any other country—take away our form of government.

OATH: **. . . that I will bear true faith and allegiance to the same . . .**
MEANING: I will be loyal to my country and to the Constitution.

OATH: **. . . that I will bear arms on behalf of the United States when required by the law . . .**
MEANING: If my country needs me, I will fight in the Armed Forces.

OATH: **. . . that I will perform noncombatant service in the Armed Forces of the United States when required by law . . .**
MEANING: If my country needs me, I will do work to help the Armed Forces.

OATH: **. . . that I will perform work of national importance under civilian direction when required by the law . . .**
MEANING: If my country needs me, I will do work in my community.

OATH: **. . . and that I take this obligation freely, without any mental reservation or purpose of evasion . . .**
MEANING: I agree that this is my choice and that no one is forcing me or scaring me into making this promise.

OATH: **. . . so help me God.**
MEANING: Let God hear my words.

Listen to Hai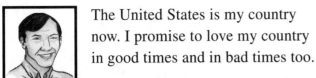

The United States is my country now. I promise to love my country in good times and in bad times too.

I hope we will always have peace in the United States. But if there is a war someday, I must be ready to help. If the government asks me to fight, I will say yes.

Maybe someday there will be an emergency. If the government asks me to help, I will say yes.

What Will Hai Say?

Do you support the Constitution and form of government of the United States?

_____ **a.** Yes, I do.

_____ **b.** No, I don't.

_____ **c.** It is the highest law.

Hai's Interview

EXAMINER: Do you support the Constitution and form of government of the United States?

HAI: Yes, I do.

EXAMINER: This is the Oath of Allegiance. Please read it and tell me if you are willing to take this oath. Do you understand what the oath means? Can you tell me in your own words?

HAI: I understand. It means that I promise to love my country in good times and in bad times.

EXAMINER: Are you willing to bear arms for your country?

HAI: Bear arms? You mean carry a gun?

EXAMINER: Yes. If the United States needed you, would you fight in the Armed Forces?

HAI: This is my country now. I stand with my country always. In peace and in war.

Listen to Maria

I am an old woman. I know the U.S. will never want me to be a soldier in the army. But I will promise to help my country anyway.

I will promise to help in a war or emergency if my country needs me.

Maria's Form

H. Oath Requirements *(See Part 14 for the text of the oath)*

Answer questions 34 through 39. If you answer "No" to any of these questions, attach (1) your written explanation why the answer was "No" and (2) any additional information or documentation that helps to explain your answer.

34. Do you support the Constitution and form of government of the United States? ☑Yes ☐No

35. Do you understand the full Oath of Allegiance to the United States? ☑Yes ☐No

36. Are you willing to take the full Oath of Allegiance to the United States? ☑Yes ☐No

37. If the law requires it, are you willing to bear arms on behalf of the United States? ☑Yes ☐No

38. If the law requires it, are you willing to perform noncombatant services in the U.S. Armed Forces? ☑Yes ☐No

39. If the law requires it, are you willing to perform work of national importance under civilian direction? ☑Yes ☐No

What Will Maria Say?

If there was a war, would you fight for the U.S.?

_____ **a.** I am an old woman!

_____ **b.** Yes.

_____ **c.** My new country.

Maria's Interview

EXAMINER: If the law requires it, are you willing to bear arms on behalf of the U.S.?

MARIA: I don't know what "bear arms" means.

EXAMINER: If there was a war, would you fight for the U.S.?

MARIA: Yes.

EXAMINER: Even against your old country? What if the U.S. fought a war against Mexico?

MARIA: A war against Mexico?

EXAMINER: Yes. Would you fight for the U.S. even if that happened?

MARIA: Yes. If I am a U.S. citizen, I have to fight for the United States.

Religious Exemptions

Listen to Susan

I want to be a U.S. citizen. But I cannot promise to fight in a war.

My church teaches me that I can follow only God. I cannot promise to follow any government. I cannot take an oath.

Two elders from my church helped me write a letter to USCIS. The letter explained why I cannot make these promises.

Susan's Form

H. Oath Requirements *(See Part 14 for the text of the oath)*

Answer questions 34 through 39. If you answer "No" to any of these questions, attach (1) your written explanation why the answer was "No" and (2) any additional information or documentation that helps to explain your answer.

34. Do you support the Constitution and form of government of the United States? ☑ Yes ☐ No

35. Do you understand the full Oath of Allegiance to the United States? ☑ Yes ☐ No

36. Are you willing to take the full Oath of Allegiance to the United States? ☐ Yes ☑ No

37. If the law requires it, are you willing to bear arms on behalf of the United States? ☐ Yes ☑ No

38. If the law requires it, are you willing to perform noncombatant services in the U.S. Armed Forces? ☐ Yes ☑ No

39. If the law requires it, are you willing to perform work of national importance under civilian direction? ☑ Yes ☐ No

What Will Susan Say?

How long have you been a member of this church?

_____ **a.** Jehovah's Witness.

_____ **b.** Since 1975.

_____ **c.** I answer to God.

Susan's Interview

EXAMINER: Are you willing to take the Oath of Allegiance to the U.S.?

SUSAN: No. My church teaches me that I cannot take any oath.

EXAMINER: Why is that?

SUSAN: Because I can answer only to God. I cannot answer to any person or government.

EXAMINER: Are you willing to bear arms on behalf of the U.S.? I mean, would you fight in a war if the government asked you to?

SUSAN: No. My church teaches me that I cannot fight in any war.

EXAMINER: What about noncombatant services in the Armed Forces?

SUSAN: You mean work for the army?

EXAMINER: Yes. Can you serve in the Armed Forces as a nurse or a mechanic?

SUSAN: No. My church teaches that we cannot work for the army because we would be helping the soldiers to kill other people.

EXAMINER: Can you perform work of national importance under civilian direction?

SUSAN: I don't understand.

EXAMINER: Are you willing to help in your community in a time of emergency—for example, a flood or an earthquake?

SUSAN: Yes. If it's outside of the army, I can do that.

EXAMINER: What is your church?

SUSAN: Kingdom Hall of Jehovah's Witnesses.

EXAMINER: How long have you been a member of this church?

SUSAN: Since 1975. I sent a letter from my church with my application.

EXAMINER: OK. I see it here. All right. You will say some things differently at the Oath Ceremony because of your religion.

What Will You Say?

Do you believe in the Constitution and form of government of the U.S.?

Do you understand the Oath of Allegiance? Can you put it in your own words? What does it mean?

Are you willing to take the full Oath of Allegiance to the U.S.?

Are you willing to bear arms on behalf of the U.S.?

If you were needed, would you fight in a war for the U.S.?

Are you willing to perform noncombatant services in the Armed Forces of the U.S.?

Would you work in the Armed Forces if you didn't have to carry a gun?

Are you willing to perform work of national importance under civilian direction?

Would you help your country in an emergency?

Your Form

H. Oath Requirements *(See Part 14 for the text of the oath)*

Answer questions 34 through 39. If you answer "No" to any of these questions, attach (1) your written explanation why the answer was "No" and (2) any additional information or documentation that helps to explain your answer.

34. Do you support the Constitution and form of government of the United States? ☐ Yes ☐ No

35. Do you understand the full Oath of Allegiance to the United States? ☐ Yes ☐ No

36. Are you willing to take the full Oath of Allegiance to the United States? ☐ Yes ☐ No

37. If the law requires it, are you willing to bear arms on behalf of the United States? ☐ Yes ☐ No

38. If the law requires it, are you willing to perform noncombatant services in the U.S. Armed Forces? ☐ Yes ☐ No

39. If the law requires it, are you willing to perform work of national importance under civilian direction? ☐ Yes ☐ No

N-400 Part 11
Your Signature

Listen to Hai

Part 11 is for my signature. I have to sign my name to say everything on the form is true. I didn't lie about anything. When I sign, I give USCIS permission to check the information and find out if it is true.

I have to sign my full name. It must be clear enough for another person to read. I also write today's date.

Hai's Form

> ### Part 11. Your Signature
>
> I certify, under penalty of perjury under the laws of the United States of America, that this application, and the evidence submitted with it, are all true and correct. I authorize the release of any information which USCIS needs to determine my eligibility for naturalization.
>
> Your Signature
>
> *Hai Pham*
>
> Date *(Month/Day/Year)*
>
> 08/25/2002

Susan's Form

> ### Part 11. Your Signature
>
> I certify, under penalty of perjury under the laws of the United States of America, that this application, and the evidence submitted with it, are all true and correct. I authorize the release of any information which USCIS needs to determine my eligibility for naturalization.
>
> Your Signature
>
> *Susan Santos*
>
> Date *(Month/Day/Year)*
>
> 09/17/2002

Maria's Form

> ### Part 11. Your Signature
>
> I certify, under penalty of perjury under the laws of the United States of America, that this application, and the evidence submitted with it, are all true and correct. I authorize the release of any information which USCIS needs to determine my eligibility for naturalization.
>
> Your Signature
>
> *Maria Elena Perez*
>
> Date *(Month/Day/Year)*
>
> 07/21/2002

Your Form

Sign and date your form.

Part 11. Your Signature

I certify, under penalty of perjury under the laws of the United States of America, that this application, and the evidence submitted with it, are all true and correct. I authorize the release of any information which USCIS needs to determine my eligibility for naturalization.

Your Signature

Date *(Month/Day/Year)*

___ / ___ / _____

Listen to Susan

My husband helped me to fill out my application. He explained the questions to me. He helped me write my answers.

I signed Part 11. Then my husband signed Part 12.

I did not write anything in Parts 13 and 14. I will sign Parts 13 and 14 on the day of my interview.

Susan's Form

Part 11. Your Signature

I certify, under penalty of perjury under the laws of the United States of America, that this application, and the evidence submitted with it, are all true and correct. I authorize the release of any information which USCIS needs to determine my eligibility for naturalization.

Your Signature

Susan Santos

Date *(Month/Day/Year)*

09 / 17 / 2002

Part 12. Signature of Person Who Prepared This Application for You *(if applicable)*

I declare under penalty of perjury that I prepared this application at the request of the above person. The answers provided are based on information of which I have personal knowledge and/or were provided to me by the above named person in response to the *exact questions* contained on this form.

Preparer's Printed Name

JEAN CLAUD SANTOS

Preparer's Signature

Jean Claud Santos

Date *(Month/Day/Year)*

09 / 17 / 2002

Preparer's Firm or Organization Name *(If applicable)*

Preparer's Daytime Phone Number

(203) 376-8295

Preparer's Address - Street Number and Name

37 LINCOLN STREET

City

BRIDGEPORT

State

CT

ZIP Code

01048

Interview Results and the Oath Ceremony

Listen to Chong

I got a letter from USCIS. It was an interview notice.

I did not have good luck at my interview. I had a bad headache. I was very nervous. I could not remember what to say.

The examiner told me that I needed to study more English. He said I could come for another interview later. I went home sad that day.

Three months later, I got another interview notice. I went to USCIS for a second interview. I had a different examiner this time. I was a little nervous, but I tried to answer the questions.

The examiner said that my English was OK. She told me that I would become a citizen soon. I was very happy!

Listen to Maria

I spent a lot of time getting ready for my interview. When I got to the USCIS office, I knew what to expect.

I was nervous, but I answered the questions as well as I could. The examiner asked me to look at my application again to make sure everything was right. He asked me to sign the application again. I signed my photographs and another paper too.

He told me that my application had no problems and that I would become a citizen soon. I was so happy!

A few weeks later I got a letter about my Oath Ceremony. I went to a courthouse to be sworn in. There were a lot of people. A judge talked about what it means to be a citizen.

Then we stood up and raised our right hands. The judge read the Oath of Allegiance. We repeated the words after him.

They gave each new citizen a Certificate of Naturalization. I will remember that day forever. It was a very important day in my life.

Next Steps

What Will You Do Next? 🔊

I will register to vote.

I will bring my sisters to America.

I will get a U.S. passport.

I will study more English and get my GED.

I will get citizenship papers for my children.

Let's have a party to celebrate!

What about You? 🔊

What will you do after you become a citizen?

Words to Remember

Study These Words

Here are some words that you might hear in an interview. You don't need to know how to pronounce or spell these words. But it is good to understand these words if you hear them. Read each word and the example that follows it.

It might help you to write the words in your own language. You might want to ask a friend to help you translate the words. Or you can use a bilingual dictionary.

accommodation
- I am asking the examiner to make an **accommodation.**
- I am asking the examiner to do my interview a little differently because I have a disability.

adopted
- My parents **adopted** me when I was 10 years old.
- I did not have a mother or father, so a new family took me in when I was 10 years old.

against the law
- Selling drugs is **against the law.**
- The government says it is not OK to sell drugs.

apartment number
- I live at 36 Main Street, **apartment number** 34-D.
- There are many doors at 36 Main Street— mine says 34-D.

apply
- I want to **apply** for citizenship.
- I want to fill out the forms to become a citizen.

Armed Forces
- Were you ever in the U.S. **Armed Forces?**
- Were you ever a soldier in the U.S. Army, Navy, Air Force, or Marines?

bear arms
- I promise to **bear arms** for my country.
- I promise that I will fight for my country if there is a war.

born
- I was **born** June 4, 1965.
- My life started on June 4, 1965.

changes
- I have made two **changes** in your application.
- There are two places where I wrote some new information in your application.

children
- Do your **children** live with you?
- Do your sons and daughters live with you?

claimed

- Have you ever **claimed** to be a citizen?
- Did you ever lie and tell someone that you are a citizen?

Communist

- Have you ever been a member of the **Communist** Party?
- Have you been in a group that follows Chairman Mao, Fidel Castro, or Karl Marx?

compulsory

- Joining the Communist Party was **compulsory** for my job in Russia.
- I had to be a member of the Communist Party to keep my job in Russia.

continuous/continuously

- Have you lived at that address **continuously** for the last five years?
- Have you lived at this address without any changes for the last five years?

country of birth

- What is your **country of birth?**
- In which country were you born?

country of nationality

- What is your **country of nationality?**
- Which country do you belong to? Which country are you a citizen of?

county

- My town is in Hampden **County**.
- My town is in a part of the state called Hampden County.

current/currently

- What is your **current** address?
- What is your address right now?

current legal name

- What is your **current legal name?**
- What name do you use to sign important papers?

date of birth

- What is your **date of birth?**
- In which month, day, and year were you born?

date of marriage

- What was your **date of marriage?**
- In which month, day, and year did you get married?

daughter

- Where was your **daughter** born?
- Where was your girl born?

dead

- My husband is **dead.**
- My husband is not alive anymore.

deported

- Have you ever been **deported?**
- Did a judge ever tell you that you must leave the U.S.?

deserted

- Raul **deserted** from the Armed Forces.
- Raul was in the Armed Forces, but he left without an OK from his supervisor.

detained

- Have you ever been **detained** by the police?
- Did the police ever put you in jail?

disability

- I have a hearing **disability.**
- I cannot hear as well as most other people.

disabled

– My mother is physically **disabled.**

– My mother is handicapped—she cannot walk.

divorced

– My wife and I are **divorced.**

– My wife and I were married before, but we are not married anymore.

driver's license

– Do you have a **driver's license?**

– Do you have a card that shows that you are allowed to drive a car?

employer

– Who is your **employer?**

– Who do you work for?

enter the U.S. illegally

– Have you ever helped someone to **enter the U.S. illegally?**

– Did you help someone come in to the U.S. without an OK from USCIS?

failed

– Have you ever **failed** to file income taxes?

– Did you ever forget to file income taxes or decide not to file income taxes?

family name

– What is your **family name?**

– What is your last name?

fingerprints

– A **fingerprint** check will tell USCIS if you have ever been arrested.

– USCIS will know if you've been arrested before because they match the marks that your fingers make on a paper with arrest records.

former/formerly

– My **former** husband was a U.S. citizen.

– My ex-husband was a U.S. citizen.

gambling

– Have you ever had a problem with illegal **gambling?**

– Have you ever played cards or other games, in a secret place, to win money?

given name

– My **given name** is Lisa.

– My first name is Lisa.

home address

– Tell me your **home address.**

– Tell me where you live.

identification

– I use my driver's license for **identification.**

– I use my driver's license to show who I am.

illegal/illegally

– It is **illegal** to drive without a license.

– The government says that it is not OK for people to drive without a license.

income tax

– I pay **income taxes.**

– I give part of the money from my job to the government.

interview notice

– Do you have your **interview notice?**

– Do you have your USCIS appointment letter?

lawful permanent resident

– I am a **lawful permanent resident.**

– I have a green card. USCIS says it is OK for me to stay in the U.S.

lawyer

- If you have ever been arrested you should talk to a **lawyer** before you apply for citizenship.
- If you have ever been arrested you should talk to an expert who knows about the laws before you apply for citizenship.

leave

- When did you **leave** the U.S.?
- When did you go outside of the U.S.?

left

- Have you **left** the U.S. since you became a permanent resident?
- Have you gone outside of the U.S. since you got your green card?

legally incompetent

- Have you ever been declared **legally incompetent?**
- Did a judge ever decide that you needed another person to make decisions for you because of a mental problem?

lie/lied

- Jorge **lied** on his application.
- Jorge did not tell the truth on his application.

mailing address

- Do you have a separate **mailing address?**
- Do you have a different address where you receive mail?

marital status

- What is your **marital status?**
- Are you married, single, divorced, or widowed?

married

- Are you **married?**
- Do you have a husband or wife?

member

- Are you a **member** of any organizations?
- Do you belong to any organizations?

mental/mentally

- Karen is in a **mental** hospital.
- Karen is in a hospital for people who are having problems thinking or understanding what is happening to them.

middle name

- I do not have a **middle name.**
- There is no other name between my first name and my last name.

missing

- My son is **missing.**
- I do not know where my son is living now.

N-400 application

- My husband helped me with my **N-400 application.**
- My husband helped me with my citizenship papers for USCIS.

Nazi

- Did you ever work with the **Nazi** Party of Germany?
- Did you ever work for Hitler's government in Germany?

nonresident

- Mohammed filed his taxes as a **nonresident.**
- When Mohammed filed his taxes, he said that he did not live in the U.S.

Oath of Allegiance

- When I became a citizen, I took an **Oath of Allegiance.**
- When I became a citizen, I promised, in front of a judge, to make the U.S. my number one country.

occupation

- What is your **occupation?**
- What do you do at your job?

only

- Was this your **only** marriage?
- Have you had just one husband and no others?

organization

- I belong to an **organization** for students.
- I belong to a group of people who are students.

other

- Do you have any **other** jobs?
- Do you have any jobs besides the one you told me about?

owe

- I **owe** some tax money to the government.
- I have not paid the government all of my taxes.

passport

- I want to have a U.S. **passport.**
- I want to have U.S. travel papers.

permanent resident

- I am a **permanent resident.**
- I have a green card, and USCIS says that I can stay in the U.S.

persecuted

- Have you ever **persecuted** another person because of religion?
- Have you ever hurt or made trouble for other people because you did not like their religion?

position

- What is your **position** at United Paper Company?
- What job do you do at United Paper Company?

present/presently

- Are you **presently** employed?
- Are you employed right now?

previous/previously

- My **previous** address was 109 Harding Street.
- 109 Harding Street is the address I lived at before the one I am at now.

promise

- Do you **promise** to tell the truth?
- Are you sure that you are going to tell the truth?

registered to vote

- After I become a citizen, I will **register** to vote.
- After I become a citizen, I will put my name on the list of people who can vote.

repeat

- Could you **repeat** the question?
- Could you say the question again?

returned

- What was the date that you **returned** to the U.S.?
- What was the date that you came back to the U.S.?

self-employed

- I am **self-employed.**
- I have my own business.

sign

- Please **sign** here.
- Please write your name here.

signature

- Is this your **signature?**
- Did you write your name here?

since

- I have been married **since** 1978.
- I got married in 1978, and I am still married now.

single

- Are you married or **single?**
- Are you married or not married?

Social Security number

- I have a **Social Security number.**
- I have a number on a card from the government. It shows that it is OK for me to have a job in the U.S.

son

- My **son** lives with me.
- My boy lives with me.

state

- My **state** is California.
- I live in the part of the United States that is California.

still

- Do you **still** live at 45 Meadow Street?
- Do you continue to live at 45 Meadow Street now?

swear

- Do you **swear** to tell the truth?
- Do you promise that you will tell the truth?

terrorist

- Carl belongs to a **terrorist** group.
- Carl belongs to a group that hurts people to get what it wants.

title

- Sir William has a **title** from the Queen of England.
- Sir William has a special name from the Queen of England.

totalitarian

- Juan worked for a **totalitarian** group.
- Juan worked for a group that hurt people, jailed people, or killed people who did not agree with them.

trips outside the U.S.

- Have you taken any **trips outside the U.S.?**
- Have you left this country and traveled to other places?

truth

- Do you promise to tell the **truth?**
- Do you promise that you will not lie?

union

- I belong to the Hotel Workers' **Union.**
- I belong to a special group for hotel workers.

vote

- I will **vote** in the election for the president next year.
- I will make my choice about who I want for president next year.

widow/widower/widowed

- Are you **widowed?**
- Did your husband or wife die?

zip code

- My **zip code** is 22435.
- I write 22435 at the end of my address.